CHANGE YOUR MIND. CHANGE YOUR RIDE.

THE MENTAL CYCLIST™

KYLE MACRAE

My grateful thanks to Marit Akintewe, Greig Anderson, Michael Band, Alex Dalton, Lois Daly, Joan Grady, Sally Grummitt, Desiree Linke, Lynne McCusker and Tom Mutton for all your support and input.

Special thanks to Misha Botting for helping to kick the early ideas for The Mental Cyclist into shape; Carrie Marshall for amazing support with writing and editing; and above to all my partner, Audrey Mason, for giving me the time, space and wine to make this happen.

First published in 2020 by:
TakeToux Ltd
Glasgow

Visit mentalcyclist.com

For Euan and Calum

THE ONE SELF-KNOWLEDGE WORTH HAVING IS TO KNOW ONE'S OWN MIND.

F H BRADLEY, PHILOSOPHER

CONTENTS

PART 1
WHAT IS
MENTAL CYCLING?

It's a different way of thinking about your cycling, and yourself, so you can do more on your bike.

Because you know what? It's rubbish being limited in life. Limited in your ambitions. Limited in your achievements. It's particularly rubbish in cycling because all the barriers we bang up against are self–imposed. They're not real. They just *feel* real.

Mental cycling is about blowing up those barriers. You'll do this by becoming an expert in yourself. This means understanding the kind of cyclist you are right now and designing the cyclist you'd love to be. I don't mean what kind of bike you have or what kind of cycling you do. I simply mean: what gets you into the saddle? Why do you ride your bike? What do you really enjoy, and what not so much?

What would you do if only you could, but don't believe you can?

PRACTICAL PEDAL POWER

Mental cycling is not about changing your personality, or balancing your chakras, or asking the universe to magically make your life better. I won't ask you to believe so you can achieve, fake it 'til you make it, or turn your frown upside down.

Nor is it about pushing your body through the pain barrier to achieve superhuman feats and break world records. You know the kind of thing: here's what Top Pro did, and you can do it too! Except, you can't. You can't because Top Pro has the best equipment, their own chef, a team of physios and sports psychologists, unlimited time for training, God–given talent and, in some cases, allegedly, a big bucket of performance–enhancing drugs.

You don't. But it's not about that. It's about changing your relationship with your cycling so you can love every ride and do anything you want to do. It's about understanding what drives you forward and what holds you back.

The Mental Cyclist is 100% practical. I'm going to help you haul your personal psychological barriers out of the shadows and into the spotlight so you can see them for what they really are. Then together we'll blow them up. Rationally. Mindfully. Permanently. Mental cycling is more than a marginal gain. It's about *change*. Changing your mind to change your ride.

I've learned that finishing a marathon isn't just an athletic
achievement. It's a state of mind that says anything's possible.
John Hanc, author

BARRIERS YOU'LL LEARN TO BEAT

While cycling is different for all of us, the things that hold us back are always the same. They fall into two camps: logistical and psychological.

Logistical barriers are *practical* considerations. Things like:

- I don't have time to train.
- I don't have the right kit.
- I don't have the information I need.
- I don't have enough money.
- I don't have any cycling pals.
- I don't have a brilliant bike.
- I don't have any bike.

We usually see these logistical barriers pretty clearly, and they're simple enough to deal with in principle. That doesn't mean they're simple to deal with in *practice*, of course. You might not have the money for the kit you'd like or have any holiday time left to go cycling in the sunshine. But you know what the barriers are and can usually figure out ways to tackle or work around them.

The Mental Cyclist isn't about those barriers. It's about the *psychological* stuff that really holds us back. These are the barriers that many of us find much, much harder to deal with. For example:

- I'm not good enough.
- I'll never be good enough.
- I'm too old, slow, fat (or whatever).
- It's too high, hard, long (or whatever).
- I'll just make a fool of myself.
- Everyone else is better than me.
- I'll feel dreadful if I fail.

Your mind is smart. It knows you inside out. But sometimes it tells you stories. Negative stories that shatter your self-confidence. Then, when you think about doing something challenging, something you'd love to do, your mind says: NOPE.

The stories aren't real. But they *feel* real. So we build psychological barriers that hold us back. Stop us doing things we'd love to do. Limit our ambitions. Affect our performance and spoil our fun.

HIDDEN NASTIES

Psychological barriers are insidious. They live in the shadows of your self-consciousness, pecking away at your belief and confidence. They tell you the worst possible version of your story. They try to stop you doing anything out of the ordinary. And if that doesn't work, they make you miserable while you do it. They tell you that everything is too difficult, too dangerous, and it's definitely going to be a disaster.

When you listen to them, this all comes true. You give up, or you don't even try in the first place. You're trapped. The way out of the trap is by listening to your mind. And, sometimes, challenging the stories it spins.

WHY YOUR MIND MATTERS

In the West, we tend to imagine our brains and our bodies as separate things. It's a model attributed to the French philosopher René Descartes, but it goes back a lot further than that. The model goes like this: we have a body to do body stuff and a brain to do brain stuff, and they happily get on with it in isolation from one another.

But that isn't true.

ALL JOINED UP

We've known for a very long time that our minds affect our bodies. That can be directly, such as extreme stress making us physically ill. Or it can be an indirect influence, such as feelings of sadness making us more likely to reach for the Jaffa Cakes. If we're experiencing depression, we may experience physical changes in our menstrual cycle, disturbed sleep patterns or unusual aches and pains. When we grieve or experience other kinds of emotional trauma, we often lose a great deal of weight. If we're really stressed, we're more likely to get the cold or suffer from headaches.

And it's true the other way around. What happens to our bodies can affect our minds. For example, when we don't get enough sunlight we don't make enough Vitamin D, and that makes many of us miserable. When the mercury climbs, we want to go outside — and if it climbs very high, some of us become more aggressive. When we exercise hard, we get an endorphin rush and feel great.

In cycling, the mind-body connection affects everything: how motivated we feel at the beginning of a ride, how much energy we put into the effort, how we deal with obstacles, and so on. A puncture is always a puncture, but it's your mind that decides whether today you're going to fix it calmly and get back on the bike or waste time stamping your cleats and shouting at clouds.

As the kids' rhyme might put it, our brains and our bodies are up a tree, K–I–S–S–I–N–G. But while they're in a close relationship, it's far from an equal one. Your brain is very much in the driving seat. And it doesn't have a neutral gear. It's either working for you or against you. Either pushing you forwards or slamming you into reverse.

TELL YOURSELF A STORY

I had a vivid imagination when I was a kid. And that gave me superpowers.

Once, I was carrying two heavy bags of shopping back home, and my energy was fading fast. Instead of giving up, I imagined that I'd heard a cry for help inside my head. My parents were being held captive by a machete–wielding psychopath! If I didn't carry the shopping all the way from Glasgow, where I lived, to London, which was 400 miles away — right now, on foot, without stopping — he'd fillet my father and make my mum into mince.

I was no longer walking home from the shops. I was a hero on a life or death mission.

PUSHING IT

Of course, I knew there wasn't really a psychopath. But our minds are powerful, even when we know we're imagining things. I gritted my teeth, gripped the bags tightly and strode purposefully down the road. How far could I go if I really had to? Would I push myself to the very limits of endurance? Would the plastic handles that were already cutting into my hands make my fingers fall off? Would I only make it as far as Manchester before keeling over, gasping with my final breath: "I tried, mum and dad! I really tried!"

Well, no. Obviously. But I did make it home without stopping or dropping the shopping, which was quite something. 'Hysterical strength', it's called. I was mainlining adrenaline, capable of extraordinary feats. I felt just like the apocryphal mother who somehow manages to lift a car that's threatening to crush a pram.

When our brains tell us stories, our bodies listen.

Train your conscious mind and your subconscious mind to start working for you by getting those great powers to move in a new direction.
Steve Backley, athlete

KNOWING YOURSELF IS THE BEGINNING OF ALL WISDOM.

ARISTOTLE, PHILOSOPHER

YOUR BRAIN RULES YOUR BODY

As any spin instructor will tell you, often loudly, when you feel like giving up it's not because your body physically can't go on. It's because your brain decides:

—		This hurts! This is crazy! I'm not doing it any more! Stop!

The pain we feel is real, but the decisions are being made upstairs. It's your brain, not your sweaty fingers, that swivels the resistance. When you ride, it's your brain that tells your legs to push the pedals. It's your brain that decides how much power to deliver, how much juice you've got left in the tank, and how you're feeling moment to moment.

TAKE THE PAIN, KILLER

How we experience pain isn't just about the messages our legs send to our minds. It's also about the way our minds process those messages. The placebo effect is a great example of that processing. If you're told you're being given painkillers but swallow a sugar pill instead, you still feel better. The mind tells the body to feel better, and the body does what it's told.

Memory has an effect on how we experience pain, too. If we've experienced pain before, the messages from our legs trigger our limbic system. That's the part of the brain involved in behavioural and emotional responses, and it helps us decide whether to battle through the pain — or throw in the towel.

Many elite athletes use mind training to improve their performance. For some it's about managing pain, which is crucial in sports like competitive cycling. But for most it's about developing the right mental attitude to deliver a better performance. That's because pros know that how they feel can have a huge effect on what they can do.

Those attributes include:

—		Motivation.
—		Confidence.
—		Focus.
—		Positivity.

We'd add one more for Mental Cyclists:

—		Enjoyment.

FEEL THE FEAR (AND MAYBE DON'T DO IT ANYWAY)

You're not a pro, but what works for them will work for you too, even if you're not competing or focused on results. If you launch yourself into a ride or a training session with feelings of determination and self-confidence, with a light spirit and positive outlook, with the self-belief that you're capable of doing what it takes, and actually looking forward to it rather than dreading what might happen, those feelings will help you when the going gets tough. But if you start off feeling anxious, believing you might not be up for it, fearing you might fail or have a hideous time, your body will do its best to prove you right.

And so you might fail. Or even if you succeed, you might hate every moment and wonder why you're putting yourself through such nonsense for an arbitrary goal. Whatever you set out to do, it doesn't matter how fit you are if your heart — or rather, mind — just isn't in it.

As I said at the outset, the key to mental cycling is getting to know yourself. It's about understanding what makes you tick and what makes you stop so you can do more and enjoy it more.

What we need here is a toolkit.

YOUR MENTAL CYCLIST TOOLKIT

Becoming a Mental Cyclist allows you to shed all the psychological baggage that holds you back. What do you need to for this? Let's start with what you *don't* need:

— Italian Lycra®.
— Carbon fibre.
— A gym.
— Keto diets, power bars, electrolytes etc.

In fact, you only need six things to become a Mental Cyclist (assuming you already have a bike). We call it the Mental Cyclist Toolkit. The first three tools are practical, and the next three are all about your attitude.

When we carry thoughts of negativity and
self-criticism, we inspire just what we don't want:
poor health and an unattractive physical body.
Dashama Konah Gordon, writer

JOURNAL

You're holding it right now. As part of your journey towards mental cycling, I'm going to invite you to complete exercises as we go along. With each exercise, you'll learn a little more about yourself. You can of course skip these exercises if you like, or just do them in your head. But you'll get the best results if you do them as they're intended.

⊥ You can download extra copies of all the exercises from the website: mentalcyclist.com/resources (free membership required).

Something else I think you'll find very helpful on this road trip to self-expertise is writing a ride report at the end of every ride to reflect on what was going on in your head at the time. This will help you develop your self-expertise in no time at all.

If you haven't journaled before, you may be surprised to discover how useful it is. It's a powerful tool for capturing how you really think and feel about stuff. And, as we'll see, for *changing* how you think and feel.

MENTAL CYCLIST MANIFESTO

The Mental Cyclist Manifesto is a 12-step program for doing more on your bike and loving every ride. It's not about hardening up. It's simply about understanding what's really going inside your head when you ride, so you can get your mind working for you rather than against you. If you follow the exercises, you'll develop:

— Awareness of yourself.
— Knowledge about yourself.
— Belief in yourself.

That expertise will improve your performance and increase your enjoyment of cycling — which you'll prove to yourself by taking on a challenge.

MENTAL CYCLIST CHALLENGE

Why a challenge? Because a challenge is a goal, and goals keep life interesting. They motivate us to get off our butts and go do cool stuff.

Now, I'm not advocating Noel Edmonds-style cosmic ordering here, or suggesting that you can make the future happen by sheer force of the imagination. Clearly, that's nonsense. What I am saying is that if you have a meaningful, rewarding and vivid challenge to focus on, you'll be motivated to achieve it.

The key thing about your Mental Cyclist Challenge is that it ~~should~~ will be something that's beyond your current comfort zone. Your comfort zone is the mental equivalent of an easy ride. It's pleasant enough and might have some sticky bits where the road ramps up or you feel a little bit tired, but it's well within your capability. It's not going to be particularly thrilling, but there's no risk of failure. If your comfort zone was a colour, it would be beige. The beigest shade of beige. The colour least likely to excite or delight, to stir your loins or set your heart on fire.

Your Mental Cyclist Challenge should be something that *does* set your heart on fire. Something that motivates you to push beyond your comfort zone. Something that makes you think you *might* fail (you won't). Something you'd really, really love to do (you will).

If you already have a challenge in mind, great! Hold that thought as you work through the Mental Cyclist. You may find that your challenge changes. If you don't have anything planned right now, that's just fine. You'll find yourself thinking of things you'd love to do as we go along, and you'll finalise and commit to your personal challenge in Part 3.

HONESTY

You're going to be honest with yourself. About yourself.

Becoming an expert in yourself requires a degree of introspection and self-awareness. You may already be used to examining your inner emotions with coruscating candour, or you may find the prospect as appealing as taking a bath in cold baked beans. Either way, I'm going to make it easy, hopefully fun, and definitely effective and rewarding.

COMMITMENT

You're going to make a commitment, and it's one you're going to love. The commitment you need for mental cycling isn't about going to the gym three times a day or riding eleventy billion base miles in winter. It's not about growing exquisite quads or refusing to eat anything Captain Caveman wouldn't recognise as wholesome.

The commitment you need is much simpler. You just need to commit to following the steps in the Mental Cyclist Manifesto and tackling a Mental Cyclist Challenge. You're going to learn to do something amazing that pushes buttons you didn't even know you had.

If you dream it, you can do it.
Walt Disney, film-maker

FOCUS

There is nothing difficult about getting to know yourself. And definitely nothing mystical. But it does require a bit of focus from time to time. To help you focus, we're going to use Three Mental Breaths.

This is a technique we've nicked from mindfulness, because it works. Whenever you need to focus, to centre yourself, you can achieve that with three deep breaths.

These aren't just quick deep breaths. They're more measured. Here's how to do them:

— Take a moment to get yourself physically comfortable. Ideally you should be sitting down with your eyes closed, but you can do this standing up with your eyes open. You can even do it on your bike as you ride, in which case definitely keep your eyes open.

— Inhale slowly and gently through your nostrils, letting yourself feel your chest and your abdomen inflate. Don't let it become uncomfortable and don't force it — we're not looking for big comedy gulps here.

— Now exhale slowly and gently, feeling the sensation as you breathe the air back out again.

— Do this two more times.

For a guided video exercise in mental breathing, pop over to mentalcyclist.com/resources.

The reason this works is because breathing and emotional states are interlinked. When we breathe slowly and gently, we're telling our brain that everything is fine. There's no danger here. Nothing to get hung about.

You can try experiencing the alternative if you like. Attempt to concentrate on something or perform a delicate task while breathing very quickly and sharply. You can't do it as well because your brain is frantically punching the fire alarm button and letting off air horns.

We encourage you to use your Three Mental Breaths as the starting point for every exercise throughout this course. It only takes a few moments, but it gets you into the right headspace to focus on the task.

You work so hard to fix yourself, but maybe what you need isn't another tactic, another book, another five-step plan. Maybe what's really holding you back is the idea that you need to be fixed.
Vironika Tugaleua, author

WE TEND TO BE HELD BACK FROM OUR GOALS BY THE SIMPLICITY OF OUR COMFORT ZONES.

MICHELLE C USTASZECKI, WRITER

CLIP IN!

For me, mental cycling was born on the slopes of Mont Ventoux. Or rather, off the slopes.

It's 2005 in the South of France. It's 35 degrees in the shade and everything is awesome. I'd been living in Provence for a year, cycling regularly on a terrible German bike with gears that jumped and brakes that barely worked. It cost me 200 Euros and weighed 200 kilos.

But while man and machine were hardly in perfect harmony, I rode it every day through lavender fields and heat-hazed hills. I'd discovered road cycling, and the love affair would last a lifetime.

But there was one hill I never went near, because it was a monster.

THE GIANT OF PROVENCE

Mont Ventoux looks like part of the moon was dropped off by mistake. It looms nearly 2km above the plains. It's boiling hot at the bottom and freezing cold at the top. Winds at the summit howl at up to 80kph. On a really bad day, they can reach 300kph. There are a lot of really bad days.

And in the 1967 Tour de France, it killed Tommy Simpson. Cycling up there was unthinkable.

"We're riding it this year and you're doing it too!" my cycling buddy Didier announced one day. The "we" referred to his personal peloton of cycling pals. These were guys I'd never met, because I was way slower than Didier and nowhere near ready for a fast group ride. But Didier was adamant: I should definitely climb Ventoux. I was reasonably fit, he said, and a half-decent climber. I should do it because it's an iconic climb that should be on any cyclist's bucket list. He told me he wouldn't take no for an answer.

Suddenly the unthinkable became far too thinkable. I couldn't concentrate on anything else. Could I really climb Mont Ventoux? Would I?

My thought process went like this:

— It's too high.
— It's too hard.
— It's way too hot.
— It's way too windy.
— I'm too old.
— I'm too fat.
— My knees hurt.
— These guys are serious cyclists!
— I'll get dropped immediately.

- They'll think I'm an idiot.
- I'll ruin the ride for everyone.
- I don't have it in me.
- I'll only fail, so I shouldn't even try.
- Maybe next year...

These thoughts weren't very helpful, but they were very powerful.

"THE PROBLEM IS ALL INSIDE YOUR HEAD," I SAID TO ME

To be fair, I wasn't negative all the time. Sometimes, usually after some wine, I'd tell myself that I could absolutely do it. I'd flip into positive thinking mode, and tell myself:

- I'd LOVE to climb Mont Ventoux!
- I'm perfectly fit enough.
- I can do it in my own time.
- It's only a hill.
- I'll feel amazing when I do it!
- Bring it on!

But those moments were fleeting and rarely lasted longer than a carafe of Chateau Chapeau. When it ran dry, I went back to pessimism. There was no way I was going to do it. So I bottled it. I told myself I'd do it *one day*. When it was cooler. When I'd trained properly for it. When I had a better bike. When I was, er, younger. The problem was simple, although of course I didn't realise it at the time. I wasn't a Mental Cyclist. My head wasn't in the right place. It wasn't even in the right postcode.

PARADISE LOST

Here's what I was really doing:

- I passed the microphone to every negative thought in my head. I didn't for a moment consider that I could influence those thoughts, let alone control them. I just listened to them and took them seriously.

- I saw the challenge as black and white. It would either be an incredible success or a humiliating failure. Getting to the top wasn't the most important thing. It was the only thing. All or nothing.

- I didn't believe I was fit or strong enough to do it. Actually, factually, this was nonsense.

- I worried about everything that could possibly go wrong. Just because something could go wrong doesn't mean it will go wrong. But try telling me that in 2005!

- I thought that if I didn't do well, Didier and his super-fit friends would see me as pathetic.

There was lots going on in my head. But this last one was the biggie. My self-esteem was on the line. Though I didn't recognise it at the time, and wouldn't have admitted to it if I had, I was equating my worth as a person with my performance on the bike. If I failed on the climb, clearly that meant I was a failure as a human being. Or at least as a cyclist, which is pretty much the same thing when you're trying to climb a mountain on a bike.

So I bottled it. I went home to Scotland, and bottled it again the following year. Then the year after that, and the one after that. Until finally, six years later, I figured out that what was holding me back had nothing to do with my physical ability to climb a hill — and absolutely everything to do with how I was thinking about the challenge.

And thinking about myself.

So in 2011, I persuaded a couple of pals to join me on a pilgrimage to Provence, and together we climbed Mont Ventoux. And I loved it! Because I climbed with my mind, not my muscles.

WELCOME TO TMC

The Mental Cyclist is the result of my journey towards understanding myself better so I could stop beating myself up and feeling like a loser. On that journey, I reconnected with why I love cycling and learned how to make my mind — my crazy, contrarian, catastrophising mind — work for me rather than against me.

I've written The Mental Cyclist to help you do the same. I hope you find it enjoyable and beneficial and go on to take on the challenges of your life, free from the psychological barriers that hold us all back. I certainly wish I'd known this stuff back in 2005.

So clip in, prepare to take those Three Mental Breaths, and let's ride.

Allez!

Kyle MacRae

IT'S YOUR MIND, NOT YOUR MUSCLES, THAT PUSHES THE PEDALS.

PART 2
THE MENTAL CYCLIST
MANIFESTO

THE MENTAL CYCLIST MANIFESTO

STAGE 1

SUPERCHARGE YOUR SELF-ESTEEM

You are a beautiful and unique snowflake. That's not sarcasm. Every single one of us is different in all kinds of ways. So why are we so keen to compare ourselves to others?

We do it all the time, in all parts of our lives. And we definitely do it when we're on our bikes. We compare ourselves to other people, and we worry that other people may be judging us. It's really draining. It puts you on a pendulum, forever oscillating between highs and lows. It's hero to zero territory. For every moment like this:

—   I am the best! I am a goddess on wheels!

There are plenty of moments like these:

—   She was faster than me... so I'm no good at this.

—   I can't keep up with them... so they'll hate me for holding them back.

—   They're all so much fitter than me... so there's no point even trying.

Unless you're a world champion, you're always going to come up against people who are 'better' than you: fitter, slimmer, stronger, faster, braver, better tanned, and way sexier in Spandex. And if you *are* world champion, the pressure's even worse because the only way is down.

YOU'RE A LOSER, BABY

Sometimes it's fine to make comparisons, of course. If you're a slave to Strava and constantly compare your stats to Frank or Frieda's, that's great — IF that's what motivates you. Maybe you'll train harder and ride better the next time around. Go you!

But all too often those comparisons sow seeds of negativity and doubt inside our heads. That's because our comparisons aren't *neutral*. We attach value judgements to comparisons, which means we make them matter to us. And when stuff matters, it has consequences.

Think back to my worries about climbing Mont Ventoux. None of my worries were actually about the physical challenge of cycling up a big hill. Not really. They were centred on how I compared myself as a cyclist to Didier and his pals, and what I thought they would think of me if I failed. I convinced myself that I'd be a burden, that they'd resent me, and that I'd beat myself up. Even if they were polite about it, they'd see me as an overweight inadequate from Scotland with ambitions way beyond his ability. Somebody to scorn and quietly nudge off the side of the mountain when nobody was looking. My self-esteem was well and truly on the line. In my head, what mattered most was whether I could keep up with Didier.

This mattered to me because if I couldn't keep up — and I didn't think I could — I'd feel like a loser. Or I'd *be* a loser, which in my mind was the same thing.

I wasn't focused on how I might improve my performance and give it maximum effort. I didn't think about how I could approach the ride with a positive attitude rather than doom and gloom. I didn't think strategically about how I might mitigate the risks of being unable to keep up or complete the climb. I didn't even consider doing it as a solo ride, free from all the pressure. All I did was think about what other people would think about me.

In reality, of course, they were much more likely to think this:

"＿＿＿＿＿＿"

Because people generally don't think about us nearly as much as we think they do. And when they do think about us, they generally don't do so in the incredibly, relentlessly, viciously negative way the critical voice in our head tells us they must.

We think they're judging us harshly. They're wondering what's for dinner.

It's a toxic cycle. Your thoughts become your worries and your worries become your thoughts.
Lindsay Holmes, journalist

Chances are you privately compare yourself with a few benchmarks in your cycling life. Friends, perhaps, or enemies, or family members, or fellow club riders, or that annoying neighbour with the ten-grand Pinarello and Rapha gear who flies up the road like a pro on EPO.

WHO DO YOU COMPARE YOURSELF TO?
Be honest — nobody's going to read this but you!

WHAT MATTERS TO YOU?
You might monitor other people's Strava stats to benchmark your personal performance, or check who's sweatier and gaspier at the end of a ride.

HOW DO YOU FEEL WHEN YOU DO WELL OR BADLY IN YOUR COMPARISONS?

This is about the emotional consequences of your comparisons. Again, be honest. It's ok to say "I feel smug when I beat Iain to the top of the hill" or "I feel rubbish when I can't beat Frank despite all my training" — if that's the truth of the matter.

The self image is the key to human personality and human behaviour. Change the self image and you change the personality and the behaviour.
Maxwell Maltz, author

When we compare ourselves with other people, we involve two parts of our psychology: our ego and our self-esteem.

Let's talk about ego first. It's often used incorrectly to describe overconfidence and arrogance, but it's actually a term used to describe one facet of our mental make-up. According to the model created by Sigmund Freud, we all have an id, an ego, and a superego. Our id is responsible for our basic primal urges, including the most negative ones. It's our caveman or cavewoman brain, focused on instant gratification and self-interest.

If the id is a wild horse, the ego is its skilled rider. It takes the primal impulses of the id and applies a strong dose of reality so you don't do anything self-destructive. If your id wants to punch the boss in the nose, set fire to his car and break all the windows of the office, your ego realises that such tomfoolery isn't going to be brilliant for your future career prospects, and reins you in.

The third part of the equation, your superego, is what's often described as your conscience. It wouldn't stop you from setting fire to the boss's car, but if you did then your superego would make you feel really bad about it afterwards.

CHECK YOURSELF BEFORE YOU WRECK YOURSELF

The ego's job is to protect you, and one of the tools it uses to do that is called a defence mechanism. A defence mechanism's job is to react to something in such a way that it stops you from getting too anxious about it. For example, we sometimes use humour to remove the sting from upsetting events or situations. That's a defence mechanism.

Defence mechanisms aren't always helpful. Your ego might decide that the best way to stop you from being anxious is not to try to do anything, ever. For example, it might persuade you that you can avoid the risk of losing a race by not entering the race in the first place. Or it might take your negative feelings about yourself and project them onto other people, such as convincing yourself that a group of super-fit kings of the mountain would leave you for dead. There's your excuse right there. Why show up when the outcome will be horrible?

That's what my ego was doing when I thought about Mont Ventoux. My fear of what the other cyclists might think of me wasn't based on any evidence, because of course I couldn't possibly know how people I didn't know would react to something that might not even happen. It was all about my own self-esteem.

You will never reach your destination if you stop and throw stones at every dog that barks.
Winston Churchill, politician

RELAX. NO-ONE ELSE KNOWS WHAT THEY'RE DOING EITHER.

RICKY GERVAIS, WRITER

We're straight into another exercise, so take those Three Mental Breaths and grab yourself a coffee. A defence mechanism is a tool that changes the way you behave, but also the way you feel. You might like to mentally climb off the saddle at this point and think about yourself in a broader context than cycling alone.

WHEN DO YOU NEED TO DEPLOY A DEFENCE MECHANISM?
When does your brain kick into self-preservation mode and throw you a lifeboat? Describe typical situations here.

WHY DO YOU FEEL ANXIOUS?
What are the risk factors? What could go wrong?

WHAT ARE YOUR DEFENCE MECHANISMS?

What do you do when faced with something that makes you feel anxious?

HOW DO YOU FEEL WHEN YOU DEPLOY YOUR DEFENCE MECHANISMS?

Relieved because you're now safe from risk? Frustrated because you'd love to be able to face any situation?

There are lots of definitions of self-esteem, but the simplest is this: it's how you feel about yourself. It's your feelings of self-worth and self-respect, your confidence in your own abilities, and your ability — or inability — to appreciate that you're capable of talking absolute nonsense to yourself.

Self-esteem is completely subjective. It's also very powerful. High levels of self-esteem have been proven to lead to better outcomes in almost every aspect of life. It helps academic achievement, relationships, happiness, and sporting performance.

WIN-WIN

The influence of self-esteem in sport is especially interesting because it doesn't just help you perform better. It makes you more likely to get on a bike in the first place.

There are multiple studies showing the beneficial effects of self-esteem in sporting motivation and achievement. Many of them are referenced in a particularly fascinating study that was published in the *Journal of Sports Sciences* in 2009. As it notes, people with greater levels of self-esteem are much more likely to take part in sporting activities than people with lower levels. And when those people participate, they do well because their self-esteem tells them that they can do well.

As the paper puts it, self-esteem is linked to "productive achievement behaviour such as increased effort and persistence." The study goes on to highlight that:

—   A strong sense of confidence has been associated with the setting of challenging goals and the expenditure of maximal effort and persistence to achieve those goals.

Let's recap, because it's really important. Improving your self-esteem improves your enjoyment and your confidence.

YOU ARE YOUR ONLY COMPETITOR

If you have confidence in your own abilities, you're more likely to get on your bike. Then when you do get on your bike, you're more likely to have such a good time that you'll want to do it again and again. If you're motivated by targets, you'll set yourself more. If you're motivated by enjoyment, you'll look for more opportunities to have a great time.

The biggest obstacle to benefiting from powerful self-esteem is the comparison trap: measuring yourself against other people and worrying what they might do or what they might think. So stop doing that. Other people don't matter.

Returning to the *Sports Sciences* paper, here's one Olympian describing his least confident career moment:

—   I was a lot more negative than I would normally be. I was a lot more distracted by other athletes and what they were doing.

And here's the same athlete taking about his most confident career moment:

—   I ignored everyone else, I was just following my routines, being aware of the crowd but not being distracted by it, not thinking "Oh who's doing what? Where am I? What's the scoreboard saying?" — all the kind of distractions which I was distracted by before. Just focusing on me and what I was doing.

As the researchers explain:

—   The athletes interviewed consistently identified confidence as a protection against negative thoughts.

That confidence also meant enjoyment. 64% of the athletes interviewed said they'd enjoyed the events when they'd felt most confident. And 50% said that when they were feeling confident, they felt much more relaxed and much calmer. The same pattern applied to negativity — lack of confidence led to increased anxiety and reduced enjoyment.

THE FEELGOOD FACTOR

Here's an Olympian gold medallist describing his best performances:

—   I just feel very relaxed, very happy with myself and happy with how my preparation has gone... you never know what's going to happen the next day but you're confident that you can perform at a level that meets your expectation.

"Confident that you can perform at a level that meets your expectation". Isn't that beautiful? As a Mental Cyclist, you should feel the same.

Mental Cyclists don't put their self-esteem on the line every time they get on their bikes. They don't waste energy imagining what other people might think of them, and they don't compare themselves, favourably or unfavourably, with other people. As a Mental Cyclist, the only comparison that matters is with yourself.

Not just any version of yourself, though. Compare yourself with the cyclist you want to be.

AS YOU THINK, SO SHALL YOU BECOME.

BRUCE LEE, ACTOR

The kind of cyclist you want to be will be unique to you. Maybe the cyclist you want to be is one who achieves certain goals but isn't mired in misery when circumstances conspire against you. Maybe you want to be able to push yourself just a little bit more than you do at the moment. Maybe you want to get a bit more enjoyment out of your rides. Maybe you want to love every ride regardless of the situation.

If performance targets are what motivate you, the cyclist you want to be may well be the cyclist who rides *this* particular challenging route, who achieves *that* spectacular time, who gets carried around on a golden throne while your rivals weep salty tears of sadness.

But even if specific achievements matter to you, it's just as important to know whether your feelings about them are wrapped up in comparisons with others. After all, you can't fully enjoy the lamentations of your rivals if you're secretly seething because you didn't win winningly enough.

Self-esteem is good not just for your mind, but for your performance and enjoyment too. The way to build and grow your self-esteem is not by avoiding the comparison trap, but by flipping it. From this day forward, you're going to compare yourself only with yourself.

You're going to design the cyclist you want to be.

You cannot change the circumstances, the seasons
or the wind, but you can change yourself.
Jim Rohn, entrepreneur

Let's give your self-esteem a boost. You may find this easy because you already know you're awesome, or it may go against the grain because you tend towards modest self-effacement. Either way, take those Three Mental Breaths and think about what you've done with your cycling so far. What are your greatest hits?

You must write three answers for the first two questions. No excuses!

THINGS I LIKE MOST ABOUT MYSELF AS A CYCLIST
What are you good at?

1.

2.

3.

MY PROUDEST CYCLING ACHIEVEMENTS
These can be big or small things. Challenge your thinking and don't necessarily go for your longest ride or biggest climb. What really matters to you and makes you proud?

1.

2.

3.

THINGS I'D LOVE TO DO ON MY BIKE

It doesn't matter whether you think you can do them right now. Or perhaps ever. Indulge your imagination and get your dreams down on paper.

— Unless you're a world champion, you'll always encounter people who are fitter, faster, slimmer, stronger, smarter or sexier than you. Don't let your critical mental voice obsess over negative comparisons.

— Defence mechanisms aren't always helpful. Sometimes they stop you doing great things.

— Improved self-esteem has been shown to improve physical performance.

— Your only competitor is you.

NOTES

Looking back over this stage, what have you learned about yourself?

1.

2.

3.

THE MENTAL CYCLIST MANIFESTO
STAGE 2

SUSTAIN
YOUR SUPERPOWER

It's 7pm on a wet and blowy Tuesday night. Sarah's just home, and she's thinking about the kit bag she packed specially this morning. She was absolutely, definitely going to go to the gym after work. But it's been a long day and it's cold outside, and she's tired, and there's a really nice Sauvignon Blanc in the fridge.

The thing is, if she doesn't go tonight that'll be two in a row. Plus a boxset put paid to last week's turbo session. While she was going to make up for it with a long weekend ride, the weather had other ideas.

Sarah knows she can't go on like this, not if she's going to do the sportive. That's only three weeks away. It's 150km, which is more than she's managed in training so far this month. So she steels herself and decides that wine can wait.

She picks up her bag, heads for the door, and mentally runs through all the reasons why she's doing this:

—   I need to be fitter so I can finish the ride in a decent time.
—   A spin class will get me back in the zone.
—   I'll feel guilty if I don't go.
—   I'll feel brilliant afterwards.

OH NO YOU DON'T...

But there's an alternative narrative revving up in her head, and it's got some very different opinions:

—   Yeah, but you're too tired to spin, so it's going to hurt.
—   You'll complete the ride anyway. Who cares if it takes you a bit longer?
—   You could stay on the sofa tonight and train extra hard tomorrow.
—   You don't have to do the sportive, you know.
—   Are you sure you really want to?
—   Just because you signed up for it doesn't mean you have to do it.
—   There's wine.
—   Wiiiiiiiine!

Sarah shakes off the voice in her head, picks up her kit bag, and heads down the stairs. She pauses to chat with her neighbour, John. "Wish I had your willpower!" he laughs, impressed with her dedication. And he's right. Sarah usually manages to force herself to do the right thing.

You probably do too. Until you don't. Let's find out why.

Willpower is what you call on to make you do something you don't want to do. The more you don't want to do something, the more willpower you need. It's what gets you up and out in all weathers, training through the winter. It drives you on when your legs are screaming for mercy. It's your personal performance–enhancing drug, your guts and glory on steroids.

Where would you be without willpower?

Willpower works, when it works, by winning a battle in your head. In Sarah's case, there was the sensible voice of a cyclist with a sportive in her sights, urging her to go to the gym. But there was a second voice with an alternative agenda. It wanted to crack open a bottle of wine and watch Netflix instead.

We call that the *Yeah, But* voice.

EASY DOES IT

The *Yeah, But* voice is smart. It knows how to push your buttons. It messes with your mindset. It throws darts of doubt at your determination. And it pushes instant gratification ahead of bigger goals.

— I really need to do this thing, you tell yourself gamely.
— Yeah, but you could do this instead, whispers the *Yeah, But* voice slyly.

See the difference there? You might find that your *Yeah, But* voice uses the second person voice and talks to you rather than as you:

— You should / shouldn't
— You can / can't
— You will / won't

Whereas your willpower talks to you in the first person:

— I should / shouldn't
— I can / can't
— I will / won't

Does that maybe suggest that you identify more closely with your willpower than with your *Yeah, But* voice? That your willpower's voice is more authentically... you? Keep an eye, or ear, out for it.

CUE THE WILLPOWER WARS

When the dialogue between your willpower and your *Yeah, But* voice begins, you're heading for a state of conflict. Only three conditions are required for hostilities to kick off:

— There's something you need to do but you don't really want to do it.
— There's an easier or more attractive alternative.
— You hesitate, even for a moment.

Boom!

Sometimes that conflict is a fully fledged fight that turns your brain into an angsty battlefield of anxiety and guilt. And sometimes it's an abject surrender where one side just gives up.

The more unpleasant or difficult the thing you have to do is likely to be, the more appealing the alternative becomes. And the more appealing the alternative, the harder your willpower has to fight.

It can be really tough. It's tempting to stay toasty in bed rather than racking up miles on a wet winter's morning just because your training app calls you a slacker. Going to a spin class may well make you fitter, happier and more attractive, but it'll never be as much fun as a pint or Prosecco and a packet of pork scratchings.

02.03 KEEP ON KEEPING ON

You probably expect to turn on the willpower tap to get to the top of a mountain when you're breathless and bonking (by which I mean experiencing hypoglycaemia because you're out of energy, not doing the other thing), but it can also be essential for more everyday tasks — like Sarah persuading herself to go to the gym. These are situations where you're doing something not because you *have* to do it — there's no gun to your head — but because it's important for progressing towards a goal. In Sarah's case, spin was part of her training programme for riding a big sportive.

DISRUPTIVE DIATRIBE

Let's imagine you're following a training plan and every so often you're supposed to do an FTP test to measure your progress. If you're not familiar with FTP tests, they're cycling exercises on a turbo trainer, Wattbike or similar torture device, designed to measure your Functional Threshold Power. This is a rough guide to your fitness level. One variety of an FTP

If you want to make peace with your enemy, you have to
work with your enemy. Then he becomes your partner.
Nelson Mandela, legend

test requires you to ride progressively harder to hit increasing power targets until you can ride, and breathe, no more. FTP tests are moderately useful and excessively horrible.

So, it's test time. Your FTP score should have increased by 5% since your last test, and you're hoping it has. You're on your turbo pedalling hard. But your legs are sore and there's a long way to go. You commit the fatal mistake of hesitating, just for a moment, and considering whether life's maybe too short for this shit. This sparks a willpower war, which you recognise instantly by the conflict in your head. On one hand, you're desperately telling yourself to do something you're not enjoying; on the other, your *Yeah, But* voice is coming up with all kinds of incredibly agreeable reasons why you shouldn't.

The deadliest foe you'll face is doubt. It's the *Yeah, But* voice's favourite weapon for one simple reason: it's really powerful. Doubts can distract you and leave you defenceless. Here's what it might tell you:

—   You don't need to do this now. You could do it tomorrow when you're feeling more like it.

—   You don't need to do this at all. You already know you're getting fitter because you've been following the plan.

—   FTP score is only an arbitrary measure of fitness, with loads of variables. What matters is how you feel and perform next time you ride your bike, not what meaningless stats say at the end of a dumb test.

—   Look, you just don't have the legs for it today. You're feeling bad already, and it's only going to get worse.

—   You can't do this, and you know it. So save yourself the effort and quit while you're ahead.

—   You're not going to get any fitter doing this test, and that's all that really matters.

—   If you don't score 5% higher than last time, you're going to feel terrible.

—   Stop!

Your *Yeah, But* voice feeds you plausible, appealing and acceptable reasons for not doing the thing you're supposed to do. If just one of those attacks hits home, you're in trouble. If you buy the argument that what you're doing is unnecessary or pointless, your willpower will wave the white flag pretty quickly. And who can blame it?

So while willpower is powerful, it has its weak spots. When you learn to recognise them, you're less likely to fall through the cracks.

To complete this short but important exercise, you'll need absolute honesty. What do you do that you don't really enjoy doing? Riding in the rain? Stretching after a ride? Training through the winter? Climbing? Descending? Dealing with mechanical problems? This is about noticing when your *Yeah, But* comes to life, and what it tells you.

WHAT DO YOU FORCE YOURSELF TO DO?
Think of some things you do that, quite frankly, you'd rather not do.

WHY DON'T YOU ENJOY DOING THESE THINGS?
Give this some thought and figure out what's at the root of your dislikes.

WHAT DOES YOUR *YEAH, BUT* VOICE TELL YOU?

Some of us have extraordinarily strong, persuasive, and imaginative Yeah, But voices. I know I do! Your responses don't have to relate precisely to your examples — just recall and write down some typical things your Yeah, But voice tells you when you're having to use willpower.

Technique and ability alone do not get you to the top. It is willpower that is the most important. This willpower you cannot buy with money or be given by others. It rises from your heart.

Junko Tabei, mountaineer

Luckily, your willpower has a few weapons of its own. Chances are you use these all the time, though you probably haven't stopped to examine what's actually happening in your head. But remember, mental cycling is about getting to know yourself better, so let's have a closer look at the things you tell yourself when you push yourself.

WEAPON #1 – LIMITED OPTIONS

Sometimes your willpower gets a boost because the alternatives are simply impractical. When you get a puncture in the middle of a monsoon, miles from nowhere, you might want to throw your bike over the edge. But after that quick blast of anger you'd still be miles from nowhere, and now you don't have a bike. You'll fix the flat and finish the ride because you have no real choice. Willpower will get you through.

Limited options are why you go to work when you'd rather stay in bed. Your *Yeah, But* voice tries to persuade you that the alternative to employment is a life of indolent luxury, but sensible willpower knows that you're more likely to end up living in a bin under a bridge. You probably don't go to work because it fills you with unbridled joy. You go because the alternative is so much worse.

Sometimes, limited options are real. But often we impose artificial limitations on ourselves. Let's say you're trying to abstain from alcohol, nicotine, computer games or carbohydrates. In our 24/7 world, it's generally pretty easy to get hold of whatever it is you're trying to avoid. To make that more difficult, you might remove all drink from your home, or throw out the cigarettes, or lend the PlayStation to a pal, or bin the bread. In moments of clear-headed courage and determination, you remove temptation as best you can, making it as hard for yourself as possible to succumb, should you crack.

Look out for that in future, and ask whether there's an alternative to forcing yourself into a straitjacket. If you *really* want to avoid stuff, do you really need to put it out of reach? Should you?

Think back to when willpower got you through a sticky situation because you didn't have a viable alternative.

WHAT WAS THE SITUATION?
We're looking for a situation where you would definitely have done something different if only you could, but you couldn't.

WHY DID YOU HAVE LIMITED OPTIONS?
What were your options, and why were they worse than the alternative?

HOW DID YOU FEEL WHEN WILLPOWER GOT YOU THROUGH?
What was going on in your head when you forced yourself to do whatever you had to do?

WEAPON #2 – PAYOFF PAYOLA

When you want to make yourself do something rather than not do something, you might limit your options in a different way. Whether it's a beer or a biscuit, you don't allow yourself to have it until you've done the thing you're supposed to do.

It's an IF/THEN thing. IF I do *this*, you tell yourself, THEN (and only then) can I do or have *that*. Nothing bolsters flagging willpower like a spot of well-timed bribery.

—   If I go to the gym now, then I can have chips for dinner.
—   If I lose weight, then I can splash out on some new kit.
—   If I sign up for this scary sportive, then I can buy myself a new bike.
—   If I get to the next hairpin without stopping, then I'll have a gel.

Is there anything wrong with this? Not necessarily, but it might make you wonder why you have to resort to *pay* yourself to perform. Does that feel right to you? Does it always have to be this hard?

In every battle there comes a time when both sides consider
themselves beaten, then he who continues the attack wins.
Ulysses S Grant, politician

Think back to the last time you promised yourself a meaningful payoff to make yourself do something tough or unpleasant. What was the if / then dialogue in your head?

WHAT WAS THE SITUATION?

We're looking for a situation where you could have done something different, but you found a way to persuade yourself to stick with it.

WHAT WAS YOUR IF / THEN DIALOGUE?

Describe the deal you made with yourself.

HOW DID YOU FEEL WHEN WILLPOWER GOT YOU THROUGH?

What was going on in your head when you forced yourself to do whatever you had to do?

WEAPON #3 —GOTTA DO WHAT YOU GOTTA DO

The third weapon you have in a willpower war is a sense of duty, or obligation. It's the difference between "could" and "should". If we feel that we *should* do something — or, better, *must* do it — then it's harder to run for the hills or stay in bed.

You're likely to feel obligation when other people are depending on you and you don't want to let them down. It's why people who train together are more likely to show up. It's why cyclists take a turn at the front of the bunch when they'd much rather be sheltering from the wind at the back.

Obligations can come with a contract or exist only in your head. They can be to other people or, oddly enough, just to yourself. The result of breaching an obligation may be severe, like being branded a lowlife wheelsucker, or trivial, like losing your job, but there are *always* consequences.

If you do breach an obligation, there's a positive payoff of sorts, of course — you don't have to do the thing you don't want to do. But any such benefits are laden with guilt, shame, self-loathing, and all that hateful stuff.

Obligations can make you feel you have no choice, and this can make you resentful and bitter. But they definitely work. They give willpower the strength to make you show up when you'd rather be anywhere else.

A useful way of recognising an obligation is by asking: what's at stake for me *emotionally* if I fail? That's different from the entirely practical considerations of being bikeless in a blizzard. It's about feeling bad because you've let someone down.

Even, or especially, if it's yourself.

When was the last time you felt you had to do something out of a sense of duty or obligation?

WHAT WAS THE SITUATION?

We're looking for a situation where you could have done something different, but you felt you really had to do this.

WHAT WAS YOUR OBLIGATION?
Why did you feel a sense of duty?

HOW DID YOU FEEL WHEN WILLPOWER GOT YOU THROUGH?
What was going on in your head when you forced yourself to do whatever you had to do?

WEAPON #4 – SELF-FLAGELLATION

What happens when your willpower lets you down as, from time to time, it certainly must?

Let's say you set out to hit a really challenging target on your bike. You want to climb a huge hill without stopping, smash your personal best, ride at a really high average speed, or do whatever it is that matters to you today. There are only two possible outcomes: success or failure. And because it's going to be really tough to hit the target, you're going to need big reserves of willpower.

But today, your willpower lets you down, and you fail. What happens next? Some people beat themselves up when they fail and get *motivated* by that:

— That was awful! I can do much better than that! I need to pull myself together! Focus!

They rise like a phoenix from the ashes of defeat, kicking back against failure with renewed gusto and commitment. Meanwhile, other people beat themselves up when they fail and get *demotivated* by that:

— That was awful! I'm awful! I can't do this! What a loser! I'm going home!

Then they get the hell out of Dodge in case it happens again.

Nobody likes the prospect of a beating. If you know you're going to punish yourself if you miss your target, this can be a powerful boost for your willpower when you're in the moment. Suffer now and you won't suffer later. But it sounds a little nuts, doesn't it? You put yourself through a present hell to avoid a future hell, both of which are entirely self-inflicted.

Of course, there's a third type of person who doesn't beat themselves up when they fail. That's because they don't recognise the narrative of personal 'failure'. This category includes sociopaths, narcissists and Mental Cyclists. We'll leave the first two categories for a very different kind of book.

A goal properly set is halfway reached.
Zig Ziglar, motivational speaker

When was the last time you felt that your willpower let you down — and how did you react? This should be a situation where you believe you could have continued physically, but your mind said: nope.

WHAT WAS THE SITUATION?
We're looking for a situation where you tried your best, but your willpower waved the white flag.

WHY COULDN'T YOU GO ON?
Describe your mindset when you decided to stop.

HOW DID YOU FEEL ABOUT WHAT HAPPENED?
Did you see it as a failure? If so, did you beat yourself up?

Willpower is an incredible force. On your bike it can help you train, ride and achieve. When you understand what weapons it has and how it uses them, you can make them work to your advantage. Anything that helps you hit your goals has to be a good thing. Right?

CRAP SHOOTING

Well, maybe. Here's the problem. *By definition*, willpower means you're in a state of conflict. Willpower is always up against the *Yeah, But* voice. It has to overcome powerful arguments to motivate you, time and time again. This conflict can leave you frustrated. It zaps your energy. As you no doubt know, the conflict frequently ends with failure and resentment. With beating yourself up for breaking promises to yourself or others. With feeling crap because you weren't strong enough to achieve what you set out to achieve.

Or crappier still because you didn't even try.

In the next chapter, we're going to look at how to reduce the need for willpower. Perhaps even remove it completely. And as we progress, we're going to challenge the binary thinking that sees cycling in terms of 'success' and 'failure'.

SOMETIMES YOU NEED CONFLICT IN ORDER TO COME UP WITH A SOLUTION.

DONALD TRUMP, BAWBAG

Here's a really valuable exercise to practise next time you feel a willpower war brewing in your brain. This doesn't have to be on your bike — you can practise it each and every time you realise you're forcing yourself to do something you really don't want to do. Tomorrow morning's wake-up alarm might be a good place to start. The more you see what's happening, the better you'll get to know yourself.

SPOT THE CONFLICT
When a willpower war kicks off, recognise the signs but don't engage. Take your Three Mental Breaths and observe what's going on in your head without picking sides. Describe the situation here.

WHY WAS IT GOING TO BE A STRUGGLE?
Remember, willpower helps you do something you don't want to do.

WHAT DID YOUR YEAH, BUT VOICE TELL YOU?
What were its most persuasive arguments?

HOW DID WILLPOWER FIGHT BACK?
What weapons were deployed?

WHAT HAPPENED?
How did the situation resolve itself?

DID YOU MANAGE TO STAY NEUTRAL AS AN OBSERVER RATHER THAN A PARTICIPANT?
It's not always easy, but it definitely gets easier with practice. Note any other observations about the experience here.

Find your passion, set a goal, go to work, evaluate, re-assess and repeat.
Elana Myers, motorcycle rider

— We all have a *Yeah, But* voice that offers alternatives to the things we know we really ought to do.

— Willpower is essential, but it has an Achilles heel: doubt.

— You can bolster your willpower by limiting your available options; promising yourself a reward; having a sense of obligation or duty to others; or by beating yourself up if you fail.

NOTES

Looking back over this stage, what have you learned about yourself?

1. ....

....

....

....

....

2. ....

....

....

....

3. ....

....

....

....

....

THE MENTAL CYCLIST MANIFESTO

MANIFESTO

STAGE 3

MAXIMISE
YOUR MOTIVATION

In 2008, I was riding the Bealach Na Ba sportive. The Bealach, located in Scotland's extreme north-west corner, is one of the UK's most fearsome ascents. In *100 Greatest Cycling Climbs*, Simon Warren calls it "the Holy Grail, the toughest and wildest climb in Britain," and awards it 11 out of 10. "Do not attempt to ride here in unfavourable conditions," he cautions. When I was there, conditions weren't unfavourable. They were actively hostile.

Halfway up, I hit the Headwind from Hell and all my energy deserted me. I could barely breathe, let alone pedal. I stopped and slumped over the handlebars in howling, horizontal rain. A pair of riders passed me, but they didn't stop. One shouted something but the wind took the words. Maybe it was encouragement. Maybe they were laughing at the loser.

I definitely *felt* like a loser. Halfway up is nothing. Halfway up says you aren't fit enough, aren't strong enough, didn't train hard enough. Halfway up says you don't have what it takes. Halfway up wants you to throw your bike off the side and get the bus home. There wasn't enough willpower in the world to get me moving again in this gale. I was losing the will to live.

I wallowed in it for a while, then I wallowed a bit more. I shouted something rude at an insouciant kestrel perched on a post, then had a word with myself. Where, I wondered, had my willpower gone?

If we consider the willpower weapons we discussed in the previous chapter, here's what was going on inside my head.

LIMITED OPTIONS

What were my options? I could lie down on the hill, catch hypothermia, and wait for the broom wagon to sweep me up, probably more dead than alive. I could turn around and ride back to the start, which was a bit more appealing but would be an abject failure. Or I could carry on, which at this moment felt completely beyond me, both physically and mentally.

PAYOFF PAYOLA

My imagination went into overdrive for a while. I made extravagant promises to myself about how I'd drink sixteen pints that night, then renew my gym membership and sign up for PT lessons so I'd never feel this bad again, then plan a lifetime of cycling holidays in benign and beautiful places so I'd never again suffer Hell in the Highlands. But I didn't really believe myself. And even if I had, deferred gratification wasn't going to turn the pedals right now.

GOTTA DO WHAT YOU GOTTA DO

Was I obliged to carry on? Well, I'd set out to complete this sportive. I'd trained for it for months and convinced myself I could definitely do it. I'd given myself a pep talk before setting off and promised myself I wouldn't quit, come what may. I felt I owed it to myself to try. But ultimately, feeling desolate and desperate, did I really care? Was it any more than a checkbox and a completion medal? Did I care enough to suffer to the top of this hideous hill and continue suffering for another 50 lumpy miles?

My pride was at stake, but... so what? I could probably live with that.

However, I was also riding with a pal, and at that moment he was some way up the hill ahead of me. Chances are he'd wait for me at the top. If I didn't show, he'd be worried. Maybe even ride back down again. Turing back was not an option. There was no mobile phone reception out here so I felt duty-bound to continue.

Which made me feel worse.

SELF-FLAGELLATION

I remember trying to flip my negative thinking into a motivational pep talk, fuelled by the fear of what I'd say to myself if I quit:

— Come on, man, you can do this. Sure, it hurts, and the weather's crap, and you feel like a loser, but it's only a hill. Push if you have to, but carry on! You can do this! You know you can! Because if you don't, you're going to hate yourself later. You know that, don't you? All that effort, all that training — and for what? Get back on the saddle and pedal!

But honestly, it's just not my thing. Failure doesn't make me want to try harder. It just makes me want to stop.

A PIE, A PERONI AND A PLAN

By the time I got back to my hotel room in Shieldaig (on my bike, for the avoidance of doubt, not in the broom wagon), I knew that I never, ever wanted to have a day on my bike like that again. Because that was just nuts. That was just miserable.

And it wasn't just today. It was lots of days. Days when I couldn't keep up with my mates. Days when my rides lasted far too long. Days when it really, really hurt. Days when I kept asking myself:

—   Why am I doing this?

Later that evening, over a restorative steak pie and several beers (not sixteen, though I'd earned them), I did something I'd never done before. I let it all out. I took some paper and a pen, and I drew a ragged line down the middle to make two columns. In the first column, I wrote down everything I loved about cycling. And in the second column, I wrote down everything I hated.

Given my state of mind that day, the second column was, unsurprisingly, a lot longer than the first.

I didn't care. Nothing was too small or too insignificant. If I felt it, I wrote it down. For the very first time, I was completely honest about my feelings towards cycling. I asked myself why I cycled at all. What motivated me to get on a bike?

That was the first step towards ensuring that I never had those bad days again.

THE PRINCIPLE OF SELF DEFENSE, EVEN INVOLVING WEAPONS AND BLOODSHED, HAS NEVER BEEN CONDEMNED, EVEN BY GANDHI.

MARTIN LUTHER KING, JR, ACTIVIST

We're going to think about the two sides of cycling: the yin and the yang, the up and the down, the good and the bad. And we're going to start with the bad, because The Devil has all the best tunes. Let's make a hate list. In fact, let's make two: things you don't like *doing* and feelings you don't like *having*. Score each from 1–5, where 1 is you don't much like it and 5 is you hate it with a passion.

I DON'T LIKE DOING
This might include riding in bad weather, dealing with mechanicals, winter training, dodging potholes, spending money on servicing and repairs, coping with horrendous headwinds etc.

Score

I DON'T LIKE FEELING
This might include fear when descending, pain in your legs when climbing, boredom when training, being nervous in traffic, feeling drained when riding long distance etc.

Score

03.02   WHO NEEDS WILLPOWER?

When you have to do something you don't want to do, sometimes willpower wins. Sometimes it doesn't. Is *sometimes* enough? We don't think so. There's a smarter way to get things done. The military calls it intelligence. We call it Mental Motivation.

You've probably heard of Allen Carr, the stop–smoking guru. He helped millions of people stop smoking (and drinking, and beat many other addictions) with a very simple strategy. As he put it:

— The key to being a happy non–smoker is to remove the desire to smoke. With no desire to smoke, it takes no willpower not to do so.

Just mull on that for a moment. It's a statement about motivation, and it's incredibly powerful. You only need willpower to persuade yourself to do something you *don't* want to do. If you *do* want to do it, you don't need willpower. If you like drinking coffee, eating cake, or riding your bike on a sunny day, it doesn't take any willpower at all to do those things. You only need willpower when you're trying to cut down on your caffeine intake, say no to the calories, or make yourself ride in the rain.

As we've seen, relying on willpower requires winning a war. So how do you remove the need for willpower and quell the conflict in your head? Simple.

— Stop doing things you don't want to do.
— Only do things you do want to do.

When you're sufficiently motivated, you don't need willpower.

Motivation comes in two flavours, and they're both delicious. Let's say there's something you're going to do, and let's call that The Thing. The first flavour of motivation wants you to do The Thing because doing so is its own reward. The second flavour of motivation wants you to do The Thing because it helps you on the way to something else.

Those two flavours are called *intrinsic* motivation and *extrinsic* motivation, although we could equally call them Jam Today and Jam Tomorrow. The difference is important.

MOTIVATIONAL MOJO

When your motivation is *intrinsic*, you do The Thing because you enjoy doing it. It floats your boat. It's right up your street. It's totally in your wheelhouse. It might, for example, be getting on your bike for the sheer joy of the ride. You don't need anything else — no performance targets, no fitness plan, no destination. This one's Jam Today.

When your motivation is *extrinsic*, you care about something down the line. It might be weight loss, improved fitness, a massive sense of achievement when you do something amazing, or possibly immortality. The Thing you're doing right now is a step, a leap or a bullet train towards your destination. You do it because you care about the end result. This kind of motivation, which takes the long view, is Jam Tomorrow.

"Nothing tastes as good as skinny feels," Kate Moss memorably, if ill—advisedly, quipped, possibly while declining a croissant. The more your goal matters to you — *really* matters to you — the easier it is to do whatever it takes to get there.

And this is your willpower's most powerful weapon of all. It's what makes doing The Thing you don't want to do worthwhile. It's the holiday you pay for by working those extra shifts. The dream house that makes the longer commute worth enduring. The near—perfect proportions you sweat through those spin classes to achieve.

It's the point of it all. It's your goal.

Your goal might be to get fitter, to achieve a new personal best, to ride a million miles, or to have fantastic buttocks. A meaningful goal — something you care about — helps willpower swat away the *Yeah, But* voice and drive you into action. You don't sit through 45 minutes of sweaty hell on a turbo for the fun of it, but if losing weight is important to you right now, you'll do it because you know you won't burn 500 calories eating popcorn and watching a movie.

I just want to be wonderful.
Marilyn Monroe, actress

IF YOU WANT TO BE HAPPY, SET A GOAL THAT COMMANDS YOUR THOUGHTS, LIBERATES YOUR ENERGY AND INSPIRES YOUR HOPES.

ANDREW CARNEGIE, INDUSTRIALIST

Now it's time to start a love letter to your cycling. We're looking for your intrinsic motivators: things you love about cycling regardless of any bigger outcome down the line. It's Jam Today all the way, baby! As before, score each entry from 1–5, where 1 is you quite like it, and 5 is you love it with all your heart. Leave the E and P checkboxes blank.

I LIKE DOING

This might include riding downhill fast, cruising on a sunny day, competing with your club, racing for segments, weaving through traffic on the morning commute etc.

	Score	E	P
	☐	☐	☐
	☐	☐	☐
	☐	☐	☐
	☐	☐	☐
	☐	☐	☐

I LIKE FEELING

This might include the satisfaction of getting lighter and fitter, the camaraderie of the road, the freedom to go anywhere on two wheels, pride in your achievements etc.

	Score	E	P
	☐	☐	☐
	☐	☐	☐
	☐	☐	☐
	☐	☐	☐
	☐	☐	☐

Sometimes intrinsic and extrinsic motivators align. It's brilliant when they do. Here are some examples.

The Thing	Jam Today	Jam Tomorrow
Go to work	I really enjoy my job	Pay the rent
Follow a tough training plan	I enjoy the exertion and effort	Climb the Col de Tourmalet
Save money regularly	I enjoy feeling secure	Retire in 5 years and raise chickens
Read a text book	I enjoy this subject	Pass my exams
Meditate	I enjoy the feeling of clarity	Increase the calm in my life
Lead a good life	I enjoy being kind and helpful	Get to heaven
Have sex	I enjoy intimacy with my partner	Make a baby

If you love your job, you don't hide under the duvet wondering if you can fake your own death to get out of the Monday meeting. Instead, you bounce out of bed bursting with *joie de vivre* and unbridled enthusiasm for a new day. There's no need for willpower here, because willpower is about forcing yourself to do something you don't really want to do — and this is something you really *do* want to do.

You can generally tell how strong your intrinsic motivation is by asking whether you'd do The Thing regardless of any Jam Tomorrow pay-off. The stronger your intrinsic motivation, the less willpower you need. You might not need any willpower at all. Life is dandy.

BACK TO REALITY

Of course, aligned motivation is not always the reality. Sometimes we're not remotely intrinsically motivated to do The Thing we have to do, and can probably think of a million things we'd much rather do instead.

The Thing	No Jam Today	Jam Tomorrow
Go to work	I hate my job	Pay the rent
Follow a tough training plan	Everything hurts	Climb the Col de Tourmalet
Save money regularly	I don't like missing out on things I could have or do now	Retire in 5 years and raise chickens
Read a text book	This subject sucks	Pass my exams
Meditate	I find it difficult and tedious	Increase the calm in my life
Lead a good life	Being good is boring	Get to heaven
Have sex	I'm really tired	Make a baby

Here, there's no Jam Today. Doing the thing you have to do is not intrinsically enjoyable, so you're not motivated to do it for its own sake. That means you need willpower to get you over the hump. Whether or not you succeed in doing The Thing really depends on two things:

— How awful is The Thing? Do you have enough willpower in the tank?

— How awesome is the Jam Tomorrow? Will you do pretty much anything to achieve this goal?

You probably don't always, or even often, think about the things you do in these jammy terms. But you should. It will really help you understand what's going on in your head.

Mindfulness is the aware, balanced acceptance
of thepresent. It isn't more complicated than that.
Sylvia Boorstein, author

Keeping a roof over your head or a nice car on your driveway is a pretty compelling motivator for going to work. But in cycling, Jam Tomorrow could be very many tomorrows down the line.

For example, let's say you're training for a big challenge and you can visualise a glorious outcome. Maybe it's hoisting your bike aloft at the Col de Tourmalet summit in the Pyrenees, joyful and triumphant. And let's say that getting there is going to take a lot of hard graft in training.

If you don't *enjoy* training — if you are not intrinsically motivated to train for its own sake — how hard will your willpower have to work between today and that summit? You need to be pretty sure that climbing in the Pyrenees is what you really want to do, because every day you train you'll have your *Yeah, But* voice right there with you, whispering in your ear:

—   Are you sure you want to do this? Really, really sure? Because you really don't have to. Want some alternatives?

ROAD TO SOMEWHERE

Think of the relationship between intrinsic and extrinsic motivation as a journey towards a destination. Let's assume the destination is important to you, so you're extrinsically motivated to get there. All that lies between you and your destination is the journey. The question now is whether you enjoy the journey.

Let's say it's going to be a lovely ride across undiscovered countryside, with a warm breeze in your face. Happy days. You love the experience of the ride so you're intrinsically motivated to take the journey. But if it's going to be a grim slog in driving rain on a dreadful road, you're less likely to jump on your bike. You'll only do so if the destination really matters to you. But even then, you won't enjoy it.

The trick, then, is being certain that both your destination and your journey motivate you. Which means having the right goals — *and* getting there in the right way.

Jam is lovely. You should have Jam Today and Jam Tomorrow. Why settle for less?

Let's continue your love letter to your cycling. Now we're looking for your extrinsic motivators, which means your important goals. It's helpful to split these into three categories:

— Physiological goals for your body. These might include achieving a desired level of fitness, improving your lung capacity, or looking good naked.

— Psychological goals for your mind. For example, improving mental health, cultivating the feeling of calm that comes from riding mindfully, or the self−satisfaction of looking good naked.

— Experiential goals for your soul. For you, that might mean the joy of a stunning view, the excuse to have cycling breaks in sunny places, or the tangential benefits that come from looking good naked.

As before, score each entry from 1−5, where 1 is least important to you, and 5 is most important. Leave the E and P checkboxes blank.

MY BODY GOALS   *Score   E   P*

MY MIND GOALS

	Score	E	P
	☐	☐	☐
	☐	☐	☐
	☐	☐	☐
	☐	☐	☐
	☐	☐	☐
	☐	☐	☐
	☐	☐	☐
	☐	☐	☐
	☐	☐	☐
	☐	☐	☐

MY EXPERIENCE GOALS

	Score	E	P
	☐	☐	☐
	☐	☐	☐
	☐	☐	☐
	☐	☐	☐
	☐	☐	☐
	☐	☐	☐
	☐	☐	☐
	☐	☐	☐
	☐	☐	☐
	☐	☐	☐

— You don't need willpower to do something that you really want to do.

— There are two kinds of motivation: intrinsic and extrinsic. Intrinsic is when something delivers an instant reward; extrinsic is longer term. Jam Today versus Jam Tomorrow.

— Some things deliver both kinds of motivation, offering immediate reward as well as longer-term rewards — such as the endorphin rush of a great ride and that ride's contribution to your ultimate goals of e.g. health, fitness and performance.

NOTES

Looking back over this stage, what have you learned about yourself?

1. ....

....

....

....

....

2. ....

....

....

....

....

3. ....

....

....

....

....

THE MENTAL CYCLIST
MANIFESTO
STAGE 4

FEEL
THE FUN

04.01 FINDING THE BALANCE

Understanding what intrinsically motivates you is essential for happy, mental cycling. But so too is understanding your extrinsic motivators. These are your goals — the end results you shoot for because there's a Jam Tomorrow payoff.

There are three types of cyclist. Which are you?

— You love riding your bike and don't much care about any grander goals. Stick you on a saddle and you're perfectly content. You're all about intrinsic motivation.

— You don't enjoy much about cycling, if you're honest, but you do care for the benefits it brings. You ride a bike because you really want to stay fit and your knees won't let you run any more. You're all about extrinsic motivation.

— You love riding your bike but you also have an eye on grander goals, whether they're indirect goals like improved fitness or direct goals like conquering iconic cols. Intrinsic and extrinsic motivation both matter to you.

The Mental Cyclist is in this last camp. You love riding your bike but you're even more motivated when you're riding for a reason.

WHAT MAKES GOALS MATTER?

There's a snag with Jam Tomorrow goals. Sometimes, we don't give them enough thought. For example, you might decide one day:

— I want to climb Mont Ventoux! That would be awesome! I'll train all winter and nail it in the spring!

Which is cool. But if you don't have a rock–solid grasp of why that's important to you, you'll give your *Yeah, But* voice a golden opportunity to wake up and start yelling at you. And it will yell at you. It'll yell at you when the going gets tough in training and you're trying to summon every last bit of willpower. It'll give you a hundred different reasons to give up, and one of those reasons will be that you never really cared about your goal in the first place.

THE RIGHT STUFF

The right goal for you must be *meaningful* and *rewarding* to you. Only that, and only you. Nothing and nobody else matters.

'Meaningful' sounds like tautology, but your goal will only matter to you if it's something you truly care about. That's going to be different for every single person, so it's important to identify the things *you* find meaningful. 'Rewarding' means it should deliver a positive, personal pay-off. Something that's tangible and valuable to you. It could be a physical benefit, such as weight loss or improved fitness. Or it could be a mental benefit, such as increased confidence in your abilities and a broader ambition to have awesome adventures. What matters is that the pay-off is something you really care about, so when you hit your goal you feel amazing.

A useful way to explore what meaningful and rewarding mean for you is by exploring the differences between performance and enjoyment goals. Performance is something you *do*. Enjoyment is something you *feel*.

FAST OR HAPPY?

Dave is 38 and he'd describe himself as a novice. He's a sunshine cyclist and enjoys getting out at the weekend if the weather's nice. He sometimes rides with a pal, but most of the time he's flying solo. He has no idea what you'd use a bike computer for, wouldn't be seen dead in Lycra, and couldn't care less about carbon fibre. Give him two wheels and an open road and he's quite content.

Amy is 27. She's a road warrior with a power meter for her bike and a turbo trainer at home. She rides with a club and she upgrades her bike more often than her phone. She knows how it feels to keep going when your legs are on fire, and she gets a buzz from big climbs. She'd sell her soul but not her winter wheels for a Queen of the Mountain on her favourite segment.

Dave and Amy are clearly very different types of cyclist. For Dave it's all about the simple enjoyment of the ride — fresh air, healthy exercise, all that good stuff. Whereas for Amy, if it's not on Strava it didn't happen. You could squeeze Dave into Castelli shorts and clip him to a Colnago, but you'd be wasting your time — he'd just take it down a country lane. Whereas Amy would ride through a nuclear winter on a unicycle if she had a performance target to chase.

Some of us are driven by performance. And some of us really aren't. Some of us love to set a personal best on every ride. And some of us just want to potter about.

BRING IT ON!

Let's look at the first kind of people first. If you're motivated by performance, you might:

— See a ride as an opportunity to test yourself.
— Set yourself a target time and speed.
— Eat while you're moving.
— Ride to achieve a consistent power output.
— Ride to stay in a specific heart rate zone.
— Push hard on the hills.
— Take risks on the descents.
— Share your stats on Strava.

If what matters to you is hitting your targets, even if it hurts, you'll be motivated to push yourself hard. This is as true in training as it is on a ride. If you're also intrinsically motivated by the process of hitting those goals — that is, you enjoy the effort and pain involved in driving your performance — then that's better still. You don't need willpower to overcome suffering if you enjoy suffering. It's Jam Today while you strive for success, and Jam Tomorrow when you succeed.

(If you succeed).

KEEP IT CHILLED

But if you're the kind of cyclist who isn't particularly motivated by performance goals, you're not going to do any of that. You're much more likely to:

— Treat the ride as an enjoyable experience.
— Stop to take some epic selfies.
— Stop for a really lovely meal in a pub with a roaring fire.
— Go on a detour to explore.
— Ride without the faintest idea of your power or heart rate.
— Take shelter when it rains.
— Get the train home because you ran out of daylight.
— Tell everyone what a great day you had.

What matters to you is having a nice time, even if it takes all day. You're intrinsically motivated by the sheer enjoyment of it all. And unlike the success/failure outcome of performance goals, it's not a black—and—white binary equation. Fun is a spectrum. You can have a ton of fun, a lot of fun, or a bit of fun. They're all positive.

The thing about binary goals — win or lose, succeed or fail, do or don't — is that they can punish you even when you do really well. For example, if today's goal is to smash a segment or ride 50 miles before breakfast, you either do it or you don't. There's no middle ground, no prize for getting 99.9% there. If you got a second-best time, you failed. If you only rode 30 miles, you failed.

Performance goals are fine until you don't hit them. When that happens, those supposed motivators can become very demotivating indeed. They make you feel bad about yourself.

That's one of the reasons I felt so dreadful on the Bealach. I'd done everything right. I'd set what I thought was a realistic goal and even drove the route the day before to reassure myself I was up to it. It felt like a worthwhile challenge to show how hard I'd trained, how fit I was, how determined I could be. I expected to feel amazing at the end.

And then I failed. I couldn't get up the bloody hill.

ALL PAIN, NO GAIN

There was no upside. I didn't even get an amazing view. The ride damn near ruined me, and I hated every second of it. I'd expected it to be tough, but in the end it was just miserable. It was miserable precisely because I never expected it to be enjoyable. It was never about having fun. So when I hit the wall on the hill, it was no fun at all. Only failure.

When you bind yourself to performance goals, you're inviting failure round for dinner. No matter how much you plan or how hard you train, every day is different. You might have an accident, or a mechanical problem, or terrible weather, or encounter other people riding like arses.

Shit happens, and you can't always prevent it from happening. If your goals are performance goals, it can make those goals impossible to achieve, no matter how you ride.

Of course, if you're truly motivated by performance goals — if hitting a certain time or distance really, really matters to you — then that extrinsic goal will help your mind power your legs. If you also happen to enjoy the effort — if you're intrinsically motivated by pushing yourself hard — better still. You're fully aligned, and you don't need willpower to overcome suffering and pain. You get your enjoyment from performance.

But you're still vulnerable, and it's important to appreciate that. Your day can only end in one of two ways: success or failure. If you succeed, you'll be happy. And if you don't, you probably won't be.

Many of us ride this way all the time. But for many of us, it isn't the best way. The truth is you don't have to care about performance if that's not what motivates you.

04.03   THE F-WORD

What if I'd been focused on enjoyment when I was riding the Bealach Na Ba sportive? What if my goal had been to enjoy the day regardless of my performance, or any targets I'd set myself? To revel in the fact that I was doing one of Britain's toughest climbs? To get a buzz from being halfway up a hill I wouldn't have dreamed of attempting a year earlier? To be grateful for the fact I was on my bike in the Highlands and not down a coal mine?

Let's talk about the F-word. When was the last time you heard a professional cyclist say:

—   Sure, I lost the lead, but man, I had so much fun out there today!

It doesn't happen often. It doesn't happen because elite athletes focus on speed, stamina and stats. For them, it's their job — and like any job, that means it's measured on performance above all else. The cycling elite compete in a field where even the tiniest gain in performance can make a big difference to the result of their race.

But the rest of us don't compete like that. We're recreational cyclists, not professionals. So for us, fun shouldn't be a dirty word. For Mental Cyclists, it should be at the heart of everything we do — because if you don't love your cycling, why do it?

SUFFERFEST BLUES

The world is full of things you could be doing instead. Things that hurt less, cost less, take up less of your time, and don't involve getting slapped in the face by inclement weather (unless you're intrinsically motivated by driving rain). Things that don't require expensive kit or weird clothes, but will still help you get fit and look good naked (assuming you're extrinsically motivated by that).

We tend to downplay the importance of fun. You're much more likely to hear fellow cyclists talk about how sore their legs are, how difficult a climb was or how hard they pushed themselves, rather than how much fun they had. For some people, fun really is the F-word. It implies a lack of seriousness, of focus, of effort, of suffering. Heaven forfend you might actually enjoy any of this!

It's nonsense. Fun is important. Fun reduces or eliminates the need for willpower, because if you enjoy something for its own sake, you don't have to force yourself to do it.

Fun is a fantastic motivator!

FUN MAKES YOU FASTER

Here's the really good news if you're motivated by performance. Fun makes you faster, because enjoyment *improves* performance.

Remember the mind–body alignment we explored earlier, where we discussed how the mind is firmly in the driving seat? One consequence of that is when your mind is having a good time, it helps you perform better naturally. And when you perform better, this helps your mind have an even better time. You're creating a positive feedback loop, a virtuous circle, a win–win situation. When you're motivated, confident, focused, positive and having a good time, you'll perform better.

—   People who do Olympic sports really, really love them. If you talk to athletes, they are obsessed.

That's what Dvora Meyers told Quartz magazine in 2016. Meyers studied Olympic gymnasts for her book, *The End of the Perfect Ten*. Quartz also quoted former Olympian Jeff Galloway, who claims that the lack of "joy runs" — runs undertaken for the sheer joy of doing it — is directly linked to the likelihood of giving up training.

When it isn't fun, people don't want to run. Having fun on your bike is easy. You just have to know what you enjoy, and do it.

The tragedy of life doesn't lie in not reaching your
goal. The tragedy lies in having no goals to reach.
Benjamin E Mays, civil rights leader

Once again, we're all about the love. We're going to look once more at the lists of things you love about cycling – both intrinsically and extrinsically – that you made in Stage 3 (WHERE IS THE LOVE? and LOVIN' IT) . If you can think of anything new to add to these lists as you do this exercise, go for it.

Decide whether each entry is a performance goal or an enjoyment goal. For example, feeling the wind on your face is an enjoyment goal. Smashing a Strava segment? That's a performance goal. A cold post–ride pint in the pub is definitely about enjoyment. Coming first in a race is more about performance, even if you really enjoy it.

First, check the E or P box for each of your answers. Then and add up the scores for all your E and P goals. Remember, you marked each out of 5. Log the total scores here.

TOTAL ENJOYMENT GOALS ☐

TOTAL PERFORMANCE GOALS ☐

TOTAL ENJOYMENT SCORE ☐

TOTAL PERFORMANCE SCORE ☐

What does this tell you about yourself? Are you more motivated by enjoyment or performance?

1995. SEVEN BUCKS IN MY POCKET. I KNEW TWO THINGS: I'M BROKE AS HELL AND ONE DAY I WON'T BE.

DWAYNE 'THE ROCK' JOHNSON, ACTOR

— Some of us are driven by performance, but others may be driven by the feeling of the wind against their skin, the selfies they'll be able to take at a summit, or the steak pie in the pub at the end of the ride.

— Performance goals can be demotivators if you consider not achieving them as a failure.

— Elite athletes don't cycle for fun. But you can, and you should. Enjoyment and enthusiasm reduce your need for willpower.

— Fun makes you faster.

NOTES

Looking back over this stage, what have you learned about yourself?

1.

2.

3.

THE MENTAL CYCLIST MANIFESTO
STAGE 5

SQUASH
SELF-CRITICISM

It's three in the morning. You're bone tired. Tomorrow's a big day. To your brain, that means just one thing. Party time!

It's a pity party, you're the only guest and your brain is on the wheels of steel. Over the next few insomniac hours it's going to play you all the classics.

— You Called Your Teacher 'Mum' in Primary Three...

— You Fell Off Your Bike At The Traffic Lights When Everyone Was Looking...

— Every Embarrassing Thing You've Done Since You Were Nine... Replayed In Real Time.

Your brain plays those hits all day long, but it's only in the wee small hours that things are quiet enough for you to really notice it. And as soon as you do, it's all you can think about. Psychologists call this self-talk. It's a constant stream of chatter. If you listened to it all day long, you'd end up banging your head with a dustbin lid to drown it all out.

MEET YOUR MASOCHIST

Not all of the chatter is negative, of course. Sometimes it's just mundane, such as "oh look, an orange." And sometimes it's positive, depending on your mood.

But a lot of it *is* negative. And pretty nasty with it. That's because we all have an internal voice that's even more cutting and self-destructive than the *Yeah, But* voice. We met it earlier in chapter 1 when it was drawing unfavourable comparisons between yourself and everyone else in the universe. Let's put a name to it now. We'll call it the *Cruel Critic*.

The *Cruel Critic* finds a cloud for every silver lining. Some rain for every parade. Self-talk is its sound system. And its favourite songs are about shame.

Your inner critic re-affirms untruths about
yourself that you have internalised to be true.
Athena Laz, psychologist

Of all the negative judgements we apply to ourselves, shame is one of the most powerful. It's the judgement that looks at a situation and tells you that you can't do anything right because you're a terrible human being. It's the emotion that tells you not to enter the race because you're not good enough, not to attempt the climb because you're not fit enough, and you'll never achieve any of your goals because you're an impostor — and everyone knows it.

BECAUSE YOU'RE WORTH IT

To understand how shame works and how it affects our motivation, performance and enjoyment, we need to understand how our sense of self-worth works. Self-worth is your mental image of yourself. Like other mental images, it's very subjective. It's not the same as self-esteem, which is how you think about your abilities and achievements. Self-worth is how you feel about your value as a human being.

In the early 1900s, the sociologist Charles Horton Cooley described what he called the "looking-glass self". His theory, which is widely accepted by today's psychologists and sociologists, outlined three stages of how we develop our internal sense of self-worth. Those stages are:

—   We imagine how we appear to other people.
—   We imagine the judgement of other people.
—   We feel pride, happiness, guilt or shame based on that imagined judgement.

The strongest of those feelings is shame, sometimes called the 'master emotion' because of its power. Shame is an incredibly negative value judgement that we apply to ourselves, often based on little or no evidence. Unlike embarrassment, which is short-lived and situational, shame can hang around for a very long time.

Shame is similar to guilt, but it's focused elsewhere. Guilt is a value judgement about something you've *done*. Shame is a value judgement about who you are. Guilt says you did a bad thing. Shame says you *are* a bad person.

DANGER: CORROSIVE MATERIAL

Dr. Brené Brown, a research professor at the University of Houston Graduate College of Social Work, has spent many years studying shame. In her TED talk, *Listening To Shame*, she explains that while guilt is positive — it tries to make us better people by making us feel bad if we do something we know we shouldn't — shame has no such upside.

—   Shame corrodes the very part of us that believes we are capable of change.

Ouch. Shame is the emotion behind the pity party your *Cruel Critic* likes to throw at 3am. It takes your memories of every unfortunate, embarrassing or humiliating thing that's ever happened in your life, and uses them to bolster its narrative that you're rubbish. Then it uses self-talk to tell you that again and again, chipping away at your self-esteem until you conclude there's no point in getting on your bike — or even out of bed — because you're just going to fail.

05.03   KNOW YOUR ENEMY

The key to getting to know yourself better is *listening*. When you listen, you can understand what's going on. When you understand, you can change. As with everything in mental cycling, it's all about self-awareness.

It turns out that your *Cruel Critic* employs four kinds of negative self-talk to make you feel awful. It's important to recognise them all, because knowing your enemy is the first step towards blowing it up.

CATASTROPHISING

You immediately imagine the worst possible scenario. You're on your bike, you see a bird, and a little voice in your brain imagines the bird smashing into your face beak-first at high speed. Catastrophising is your personal voice of doom, constantly predicting imminent Armageddon.

I'm a world-class catastrophist. It stems from childhood, when I figured out that if I always imagined the worst-case scenario coming true, I could never be disappointed. I could only be pleasantly surprised if it didn't happen. It's a terrific strategy that I highly recommend. Life is a series of upsides, because things seldom turn out quite as bad as they could. Then again, you do have to go through life constantly preparing for the worst, which is pretty exhausting and depressing. So, maybe not.

RE-RUNNING

You replay things that have already happened. Sometimes you do it because it can help make sense of an event. But a lot of the time it's just another way for the *Cruel Critic* to bring out its record collection and remind you of what Tina Walker said about halitosis when you were seven.

REHEARSING

This is your brain's attempt to predict the future by imagining it happening. When rehearsing is positive, it can be really good for us. There's stacks of research that shows the beneficial effects of mental rehearsal and visualisation for improving sporting performance. But it can all too easily become catastrophising, when your expectation of a pleasant ride in the sun is suddenly overcome by apocalyptic imaginations of feathery-faced fiascos.

BLAMING

This is when you try to pin everything on an individual or on some sinister force. Often the person you blame is yourself.

05.04   MISERY LOVES COMPANY

Your *Cruel Critic's* relentless negativity can involve more than one kind of self-talk. For example, if you're preparing for a cycling event, your day may well go like this:

—   Re-running previous events that didn't go well.
—   Catastrophising to come up with the worst possible things that could happen this time.
—   Rehearsing the worst-case scenario again and again.
—   Starting the event in a miserable, negative frame of mind.
—   Making a complete arse of things.
—   Blaming yourself for being a loser.

Imagine that your *Cruel Critic* wasn't your own brain, but a friend sitting next to you and nipping away for hours, telling you in great detail just how awful you are, how hopeless you've been at everything you've ever done, how humiliating the next few hours are going to be, and how there's no point in you ever trying anything because you're such a waste of space.

You wouldn't take it from a friend, would you — so why do you take it from yourself? And yet when it's your *Cruel Critic*, your personal purveyor of fake news, you don't just share the sofa and snuggle up. You get out the good duvet cover and the special biscuits, and invite them to stay for eternity.

What do you tell yourself when your *Cruel Critic* gets into its stride? And how do you feel and react as a result? This exercise is useful after every ride and training session. There's always the prospect of a bath or a beer to enjoy post–ride, but getting up close and personal with your *Cruel Critic* is really important. Do it in the bath with a beer if you like, but definitely do it. When you reflect on your experiences and identify your triggers, you can begin to unlearn the beliefs that lead you to make negative value judgements.

WHAT ARE YOUR TRIGGERS FOR NEGATIVE SELF-TALK?

A trigger is what sets your cruel critic off on one of its diatribes. They're different for everyone. Your triggers may be pain from pushing yourself harder than usual, missing a performance target, the frustrations of a mechanical issue, a sudden change in the weather, or pretty much anything that happens on a bike. Focus on your top three triggers.

1. _____

2. _____

3. _____

WHAT DOES YOUR CRUEL CRITIC TELL YOU?
When you're riding, use your Three Mental Breaths to bring yourself fully into the moment: then listen to what's being said in your head. Don't worry about whether the self–talk is true or false, rational or irrational.

_____

_____

_____

_____

_____

_____

_____

_____

HOW DOES YOUR CRUEL CRITIC MAKE YOU FEEL?

Not great, for sure — but try to be specific about the emotions you experience when you're dealing with negative self-talk.

HOW DOES YOUR CRUEL CRITIC AFFECT YOUR BEHAVIOUR?

A change in your emotional condition can have consequences for your ride. Note any changes in your behaviour.

We become what we think about.

Earl Nightingale, author

05.06   RESPECT YOURSELF

Our brains are great at all kinds of things, but predicting the future is not one of them. If its predictions were reliable, every public speaker would finish their speech with their trousers at their ankles or their skirt tucked into their tights, while bored audience members threw paper aeroplanes, or worse, at them. Every work of art would see its creator chased through town by angry yokels waving pitchforks and lighted torches.

And no sportsperson would ever win anything at all.

SPINNING IN CIRCLES

We *know* this, and yet we still listen to, and believe, a relentless negative narrative. And of course, this creates a self-fulfilling prophecy. When you tell yourself you can't do it, you vastly increase the likelihood that you *won't* do it. Which reaffirms your appalling ineptitude, and makes it almost certain you won't believe you can do it next time around either.

Now you have a vicious circle to contend with. The Staple Singers expressed it beautifully in their 1972 hit Respect Yourself, which suggested:

—   If you don't respect yourself, ain't nobody gonna give a good cahoot.

Or, as author and civil rights activist Maya Angelou so memorably put it:

—   If I am not good to myself, how can I expect anyone else to be good to me?

Being good to yourself sounds like a good idea, right? And it is, because (spoiler alert) treating yourself with self-respect rather than self-criticism removes so much stress, anxiety, and negativity from your life at a stroke.

There are two steps to dealing with the *Cruel Critic*. First, you're going to prove that you're stronger than it is with an exercise in positive thinking. And then we're going to explore three ways of keeping it under control.

YOU'VE BEEN CRITICIZING YOURSELF FOR YEARS AND IT HASN'T WORKED. TRY APPROVING OF YOURSELF AND SEE WHAT HAPPENS.

LOUISE HAY, MOTIVATIONAL SPEAKER

In this exercise, you're going to visualise the cyclist you want to be. There's only one rule: you can only use positive words and phrases. What emerges when you focus on the positive and don't leave any room for self-criticism?

If you're British, this may feel quite unnatural. We're not often encouraged to flatter ourselves. But we can change that right here. It's important to do so, because if we don't know who we want to be, we can't work out how we're going to get there — or know when we've arrived. And, of course, this is solely between yourself and your journal, so you don't need to worry about anybody else seeing what you're writing. Be positive, and be bold!

Start with a positive I AM statement, then build on it with a future-gazing statement about how you could be even better. Repeat until you feel awesome :)

I AM

I WILL BE

I AM

I WILL BE

I AM

I WILL BE

I AM

I WILL BE

I AM

I WILL BE

I AM

I WILL BE

I AM

I WILL BE

I AM

I WILL BE

I AM

I WILL BE

I AM

I WILL BE

I AM

I WILL BE

I AM

I WILL BE

I AM

I WILL BE

Have you ever used noise–cancelling headphones? They feel a little like magic in the way they silence background noise, such as aeroplane engines or train noise, but they're a lot more scientific than that. They work by producing a mirror image of what's going on. The sound we hear is made up of audio waves, and you can cancel out an audio wave by generating an identical but negative version of the same wave at the same frequency. If the original wave goes up and your wave goes down in perfect symmetry, when you combine them the waves disappear and are replaced with a flat line.

Silence.

SQUARE GO

For some people, the same thing works with the *Cruel Critic*. When it goes low, they go high. When it says up, they say down. When it says nope, they shout back:

—   Hell yeah!

Positive affirmation is a technique taken straight from Cognitive Behavioural Therapy, where you actively replace negative thoughts with positive ones. When you hear the voice of doom, you counter it with the precise opposite:

—   I CAN do this.
—   I WILL achieve that.
—   I AM up for this.

Here's Vincent Van Gogh, whose headphones would have fallen off anyway:

—   If you hear a voice within you say 'you cannot paint', then by all means paint, and that voice will be silenced.

KEEP IT POSITIVE

There was a fascinating study of marathon runners (*Van Raalte, Morrey, Cornelius and Brewer, 2015*), whose sport — like cycling — gives them lots of time to talk to themselves. Of nearly 500 elite and amateur runners, 88% reported using self–talk. 43% of the elite runners and 31% of the others said they used *positive* motivational self–talk ("You can do it!"), while just 8% of the elite runners used *negative* self–talk ("Don't fail!").

Another key finding was that the runners often use self-talk for smaller objectives rather than the entire marathon. They would focus not on the entire 26 miles but on the next mile marker, or on maintaining a particular speed for a certain amount of time.

43% of the elite runners focused their self-talk on the process of running — the length of their stride, their pace, their form, and so on — compared to 18% of the others. That kind of self-talk is known as associative self-talk, because it's associated with what you're doing. The other kind, dissociative self-talk, is when you tune out. You think about what's for dinner, or sing a song in your head, or plan terrible things you're going to do to your enemies. That kind of self-talk is less effective when it comes to performance.

There was another interesting finding. None of the runners talked to themselves about quitting the race, not even in terms of "I will not quit". That's because when you try not to think about something, it's all you can think about.

ALLOW YOURSELF TO BELIEVE

Writing positive affirmations to counter your negative thinking is a great start, and you're about to do it. But to make them stick, you have to believe in the positives. For most of us, this means *allowing* ourselves to believe. It's a bigger step than it sounds. When you're used to your *Cruel Critic* putting you down, it takes focus and practice to change your thinking.

So say your affirmations out loud. Repeat them to yourself on the bike, in the car, in the shower, in your bed. Embed them as part of who you are and accept that they are valid and powerful. You don't necessarily need to park yourself in front of the mirror and intone, "I am special and beautiful and each and every day I am growing in every possible way." Though if that works for you, go for it. It's more important to listen out for the *Cruel Critic* beginning its nonsense, and actively cross out the negatives as they arise with a mental marker pen.

Drag your thoughts away from your troubles... by the ears, by the heels, or any other way you can manage it.
Mark Twain, author

Whenever your internal *Cruel Critic* starts its nonsense, take every negative statement or thought and flip it. Find the opposite. Replace negative self-talk with positive affirmations. For example, if your *Cruel Critic* tells you that you're not up to it, the converse is to affirm that you're very much up to it. When the *Cruel Critic* makes you doubt yourself, focus on your confidence instead. A good starting point is when you captured some of your negative self-talk earlier. Revisit that now, and let it guide your statements below.

START WITH THE NEGATIVE

Write up to 5 negative statements about yourself as a cyclist. If you sometimes judge yourself harshly, get it down in writing here. If you think you're a quitter, say so. If you wish you were more motivated to get fit, capture that here.

1. _____

_____

2. _____

_____

3. _____

_____

4. _____

_____

5. _____

_____

FLIP TO THE POSITIVE

Now write the opposite statement. This can be as simple as removing negative words like NOT and replacing DON'T with DO. How does it feel when you switch the negatives to positives? Good? Good! Keep doing it.

1.

2.

3.

4.

5.

Some people find that a more visceral and aggressive approach suits them better than reasoned affirmations. A mantra is essentially a positive affirmation that's framed as a statement — or command — in its own right. If your *Cruel Critic* is a distracting heckler, an affirmation will counter it with opposing views. A mantra will shout, or shoot, it down.

A great example is cycling legend Jens Voight, whose "Shut up, legs!" mantra became his brand. His legs hurt as much as the next man's in the peloton, but he refused to allow pain to affect his performance.

MAN UP WITH MANTRAS

Mantras work brilliantly for some people, and we strongly encourage you to give this technique a go. They're best served cold, in the sense that you should choose what you'll need for the day and use your mantras consistently from the start. The trick is to repeat them frequently as you ride — say them again, and again, and again. The more you say them, the more you'll believe them. The more you believe them, the better your body will respond. Mantras are less successful if you get yourself in a pickle during the ride and start screaming at yourself to man up. A mantra is not a magic bullet. It's not even a power gel.

You need to create your own mantras. The more they mean to you, the more powerful they will be. Here are some of mine. Note that unlike positive affirmations, I always talk to myself using the second person voice ('you' rather than 'I'). I find I listen to myself more that way. Weird, I know.

— You've got this.
— Your legs are strong today.
— You're not going to stop.
— You're doing ok.
— You're lucky and loving this.
— Enjoy, don't endure.

As with other aspects of mental cycling, what works for you might not be what works for anybody else. Bellowing "My legs are strong!" inside your head could be just the tonic for you when the *Cruel Critic* tries to convince you to climb off your bike and curl up in a ditch. Try it and see.

EVERY DAY YOU MUST UNLEARN THE WAYS THAT HOLD YOU BACK. YOU MUST RID YOURSELF OF NEGATIVITY, SO YOU CAN LEARN TO FLY.

LEON BROWN, BASEBALL PLAYER

Have some fun with this! You know what you need to tell yourself, so get it down on paper. A good way to start is by looking at your positive affirmations and turning them into commands, or imperatives. So "I am a fighter, not a quitter" could become "You will not quit".

PUT ALL EXCUSES ASIDE AND REMEMBER THIS: YOU ARE CAPABLE.

ZIG ZIGLAR, MOTIVATIONAL SPEAKER

05.09 MINDFULNESS

In the practice of mindfulness, our thoughts and feelings don't define us, and they don't control us. They are not what we are — they're just things that we happen to be thinking and feeling at a particular time. We can notice them and see or hear them for what they really are — just passing thoughts and feelings. They have no power, and they don't deserve to be indulged. There's a world of difference between:

—   I want to die!

And:

—   I notice that I'm feeling tired and sore right now.

With a mindful approach, you don't try to silence your self-criticism. Instead, distance yourself from the present emotion and don't engage with it. You step back and notice what's going on in your mind and body, rather than react to it. You don't try to win a battle in your head with positive affirmations or shouty mantras. You simply avoid the conflict.

BODY SWERVE WITH YOUR MIND

Now, many millions of words have been written about mindfulness. One thing is certain: it takes practice and time for it to feel natural, and to achieve meaningful results. But if you do manage to quietly observe your thoughts and feelings rather than engage with intent, eventually your *Cruel Critic* won't bother you nearly so much.

And that's a massive win for your cycling and your life.

MINDFULNESS MEANS BEING AWAKE. IT MEANS KNOWING WHAT YOU ARE DOING.

JON KABAT-ZINN, STRESS REDUCTION CLINIC

The best way to make mindfulness a part of your life is to follow a course. I'm a huge fan of Headspace, the meditation app, for example. However, I believe it's possible to learn one core technique quite quickly — and to benefit from it whenever you hear the *Cruel Critic* whisper negativity in your inner ear. With a mindful approach, you can let such thoughts pass through you without reacting to them.

It's helpful to follow a guided practise, so I've prepared one for you on The Mental Cyclist website (mentalcyclist.com/resources). Here's the executive summary:

—   Sit or lie comfortably. If sitting, straighten your upper body, but don't stiffen it. Drop your head a little bit so your neck isn't working too hard.

—   Take Three Mental Breaths and relax.

—   Continue to breathe deeply, and focus on your breathing.

—   Notice any thoughts and feelings, but don't react to them. They're just thoughts, just feelings.

—   When you find yourself focusing on a thought or feeling, bring your attention back to your breathing. Repeat your Three Mental Breaths. Let everything else come and go.

—   Make some notes here about how you felt during the session. In particular, how easy or difficult did you find it to let your thoughts and feelings flow?

—   Repeat frequently.

NOTES

— The key to improving your sense of self-worth is to recognise when your internal *Cruel Critic* is trying to bring you down.

— You wouldn't talk to any of your friends the way your *Cruel Critic* talks to you — and you don't have to take it from yourself.

— Several tools can help you silence your *Cruel Critic*: affirmations, mantras, and mindfulness.

NOTES

Looking back over this stage, what have you learned about yourself?

1.

2.

3.

THE MENTAL CYCLIST MANIFESTO

STAGE 6

BIN THOSE
LIMITING BELIEFS

Limiting beliefs stop us doing things we might otherwise do, because we don't believe we can do them. Things like:

— I shouldn't get up to dance, because I'm a really bad dancer.

— There's no point going for promotion, because I won't get it.

— I can't ask that person on a date, because they're out of my league.

— I can't go up there, because I'm scared of heights.

— I shouldn't take that course, because it'll be too difficult for me.

— I can't go out on my bike, because I just don't have the time.

— I don't deserve nice things, because I'm a terrible person.

— I shouldn't join a club, because I'm too inexperienced.

— I can't ride in winter, because I'm miserable when I'm cold.

— I don't push myself hard enough on big rides, because I don't like pain.

— I can't do the challenge, because I don't have what it takes for something like that.

— I won't train enough, because I'm a bit lazy.

— I can't buy the bike I'd really like, because I'm a bit skint.

— I feel embarrassed in Lycra, because I'm too heavy.

— I should avoid downhill runs, because I'm scared of falling off.

— There's no point trying to lose weight, because I can never sustain a diet.

— I won't sign up for that sportive, because I'll end up getting dropped and riding alone.

— I can't sit down, because my buttocks are made of glass.

I'm not making that last one up. Somewhere between the 15th and 17th century, lots of people in Europe were convinced that they were made of glass. The most famous sufferer of the 'glass delusion' was King Charles VI of France, who wore reinforced pants to protect himself from accidental shattering. His belief was apparently sincere, and very definitely limiting.

To change a habit, make a conscious
decision, then act out the new behaviour.
Maxwell Maltz, author

Chances are you don't think your bum's made of glass but you will have limiting beliefs of your own. What all limiting beliefs have in common is a simple formula:

—   I can't do X, because Y.

> I can't.
>> I can't.
>>> I can't.

That's your *Cruel Critic* in full flow, using your limiting beliefs for fuel.

06.02   DANCE THE CAN CAN!

Mental cycling is about c*a*n. It's time to change your mind so you can change your ride. Now, this isn't about flipping your thinking into a magical 'positive mental attitude'. You know the cliché:

—   You won't achieve if you don't believe.

Is that true? Sure, sometimes. If the achievement you're shooting for lies on the very outskirts of your comfort zone, you need to believe you can get there or else the chances are you'll just stop. No point wasting energy and effort on something you think is beyond your reach. But that doesn't mean you will achieve whatever you want *simply* by believing you can do it, as many a self-help guru would have you, er, believe. Self-belief might be a *necessary* ingredient for success, like eggs in a pancake recipe. But it's not a *sufficient* ingredient. You also need sugar and flour.

I BELIEVE I CAN FLY

Most of us know people whose opinion of their own abilities or talent bears no relation to the facts. If you can't think of anybody off-hand, turn on any reality TV programme and marvel at the parade of delusional nobodies, chock-full of self-belief but utterly devoid of talent. All the iron-clad bulletproof unquestioning self-belief in the world will only get you so far if your house is built on hubris.

So it's not enough to flip a switch and cry: "Hell, yes, of course I can do it! I can do anything! Bring it on!" Because that might be delusional. If it is, you'll fail at whatever you set out to do. Then when you fail, you'll feel awful and be demotivated to take on anything else. And we don't want that, do we?

This chapter goes deeper than finding strategies for dealing with the *Cruel Critic*. This isn't about fighting back with affirmations or mantras, nor about letting negative thoughts pass without judgement. This is about gaining the self-knowledge to understand what lets your personal *Cruel Critic* out of its box in the first place — and rationally, permanently, shoving it back in and locking the lid.

WHAT MATTERS, MATTERS

So let's get those limiting beliefs out in the open once and for all. We'll figure out whether each limiting belief is actually true, so you can ditch the ones that aren't. That's really liberating, I promise. Then you'll decide whether those that remain really matter to you. If they don't matter, great — you'll bin them too. If they do matter, that's fine. You'll change them so they're no longer true, or adapt your goals so they no longer matter.

06.03   BELIEVE IT OR NOT

Is believing something the same as knowing it? What makes you so sure that you have legs, or that the air is breathable, or that gravity stops you floating off into space? Do you *know* these things, or believe them?

We often confuse belief with knowledge but in fact they're different, and the distinction is important. You can believe something that isn't true. For example, some people believe the Earth is flat. There's no evidence for it and it's demonstrably untrue, but you can believe it if you want. However, there's no meaningful sense in which you can be said to *know* that the Earth is flat. Except in your own head, perhaps, but if you're a flat-Earther you have bigger problems than epistemology to worry about.

DODGY LOGIC

Conversely, you can disbelieve things that are true. Some people don't believe Neil Armstrong ever set foot on the Moon, even though it's true and there's evidence to prove it. You may not believe that you are a wonderful person despite a similar wealth of evidence to the contrary.

In order for you to *know* something, three factors must align:

—   There's sound evidence for it.
—   It's true.
—   You believe it.

Knowledge is often defined as 'justified true belief'.

By far, the strongest form of evidence for beliefs is personal experience. For example, if you've been bitten by a dog then of course you're going to be more wary around dogs in future. You've developed a belief that dogs are bitey things.

But it's easy for us to make faulty decisions based on our personal experiences. If 100% of the dogs you've met so far have bitten you, it's perfectly reasonable for you to think you know that every dog you encounter in the future will bite you too. So you'll probably avoid dogs. That particular limiting belief may be understandable, but it isn't true.

We can also be misled by others. No matter how worldly or clever we are, we can't know or experience everything; we have to get a lot of our evidence from third parties. Unfortunately not all of that evidence is true. Air travel is much safer than car travel, but car crashes aren't given the same blanket news coverage as air crashes. So while it's understandable if you're one of the many people more scared of getting on a plane than of driving to the airport, once again it's a limiting belief that isn't backed up by the facts.

And of course, limiting beliefs are as much about ourselves as they are about external things such as angry dogs or transport disasters. We often believe very negative things about ourselves, even if the facts prove otherwise.

As a Mental Cyclist, it's important to ask two questions:

1.   Is your limiting belief justified and true? That is, do you *know* this thing about yourself?

2.   Does your limiting belief matter?

The best way to explore this is through some examples. We'll follow these with a pretty detailed exercise that will help you find your own limiting beliefs, work out whether they're true, and decide whether they matter.

It's not who you are that holds you
back. It's who you think you're not.
Denis Waitley, motivational speaker

JOSH DOESN'T BELIEVE HE CAN WIN THE WORLD HOUR RECORD

Josh doesn't think he can be the fastest rider in the world. He absolutely believes this one. Let's ask the first question:

—   Does he know this?

The short answer is yes. He knows it because he's 46 years old, 85 kilos, and strictly amateur. He's looked at the people who have won the WHR, at their training regimes and their equipment, and he knows that unlike, for example, 2019 winner Victor Campenaerts, he not only lacks the right training regime or the opportunities to follow a similar one, but also has no chance of getting a Ridley Arena Hour Record bike with custom handlebar extensions specifically moulded for his forearms, aero paint and carbon disc wheels. In other words, he has as much chance of setting a new WHR as he has of being asked to join Little Mix as a backing dancer.

So this belief is justified and true, because it's backed by sound thinking and evidence. Josh is right to believe he can't win the WHR, and it's fair to say he knows he can't. It's a fact. So let's ask the second question:

—   Does it matter?

No, not in the least, because Josh has no intention of trying. He's sane enough to know it would be easier to set himself the challenge of cycling on the moon. The dark side.

JOSH DOESN'T BELIEVE HE'S FIT ENOUGH TO RIDE THE MALLORCA 312

The Mallorca 312 is an incredibly tough endurance event that involves riding 312km with 5,000m of climbing in a single day. Whenever you read about it, you'll encounter cheerful words such as "gruelling", "savage", "grim", and "a world of pain". There's a cut-off time of 14 hours, which means riding at an average of 14 mph / 22 kph. That's not including breaks.

Josh doesn't think he can do it.

—   Does he know this?

Well, now. Josh thinks he's probably not fit enough. And he probably doesn't have time to train for it, because the event is only three months away. He thinks it's probably beyond his ability even if he did time to train properly.

But did you spot the repeated use of the word 'probably'? Probably isn't evidence. It's supposition. If Josh had a heart condition that would kill him if he tried a 312km endurance ride, then trying it would definitely be a bad idea. If he was 86 instead of 46, he'd be smart to stay at home. But he doesn't have a heart condition and he isn't 86. All he has is a lack of peak fitness and a bunch of assumptions and doubts. A whole lot of 'probably'. What's going on here isn't knowledge. It's belief. In the absence of rock-solid evidence and justification, Josh is jumping straight to a limiting belief. I can't do it, he says. He thinks he knows he can't do it, but he's wrong.

—   Does it matter?

Yes, this time it *does* matter, because he's holding himself back from doing something he might love. Josh could spend the next six years wishing he had entered the Mallorca 312, just as I wished I had climbed Mont Ventoux. Don't do that, Josh. It's daft.

JOSH THINKS HE'S TERRIBLE AT DESCENDING

Josh has a fear of heights. This isn't helpful when he finds himself riding downhill fast on the edge of a cliff with a drop-off to certain death on the other side of a low wall that's exactly the right height to catapult him over the top. But even when the road is relatively safe and his vertigo not an issue, he lacks the bike-handling skills to descend safely at speed. So he tenses up in the saddle, clings to the brakes, prays that his tyres don't explode because the rims overheat, and endures the descent in a sweaty state of fear and loathing.

—   Does he know this?

Yes. As a matter of fact, not opinion, Josh has never learned the skills of descending with confidence. That's not to say he'd crash if he really went for it. But he might. For example, since he always takes bends pretty wide, he could easily smash into an oncoming car if he lost control for just a moment. Plus his fear of heights makes certain roads very challenging indeed.

—   Does it matter?

Yes, because Josh wants to enjoy all of his cycling. He's a decent climber and he'd like to get down the other side with enjoyment rather than terror. That's all. He doesn't need to be a daredevil descender, scything through switchbacks hunched on his top tube like a pro. He just wants to go down safely, somewhat faster than he goes up, and experience the same kind of exhilaration that his mates feel.

The mind is the limit. As long as the mind can envision the fact that you can do something, you can do it, as long as you really believe 100 percent.
Arnold Schwarzenegger, actor

In this exercise, you're going to frame every negative thing you say about yourself as a limiting belief, using the format: I can't do X, because Y.

You can approach this from either direction. First, write down any limiting beliefs you're aware of in the Y column, and work out exactly what they stop you doing. Any limiting belief can stop you doing lots of things, so there's space here for three X factors for every Y factor. Once you've done that, think about anything else you can't or don't do right now, and put it in the X column. Then work out why you can't or don't do it. Is there a limiting belief at work? Pop it in the Y column.

WHAT ARE YOUR LIMITING BELIEFS, AND WHAT ARE THE CONSEQUENCES?
You might want to turn back to Stage 5 to revisit your Cruel Critic before you begin.

I CAN'T DO X:

....

....

....

BECAUSE Y:

....

....

....

I CAN'T DO X:

....

....

....

BECAUSE Y:

....

....

....

I CAN'T DO X:

....

....

....

BECAUSE Y:

....

....

....

I CAN'T DO X:	**BECAUSE Y:**

I CAN'T DO X:	**BECAUSE Y:**

ARE YOUR LIMITING BELIEFS TRUE?

Look at each of your limiting beliefs and ask yourself honestly: is it true? Really? Sometimes the act of writing it down is enough to help you see that what you think you believe isn't actually justified and true. Draw a line through any limiting beliefs you're happy to discard. You should be left only with limiting beliefs you firmly believe to be true.

DO YOUR LIMITING BELIEFS MATTER?

Now ask yourself: how much do you care about the things that these limiting beliefs stop you from doing? Score out any that don't really matter to you. You should now be left only with limiting beliefs you firmly believe to be true and have consequences that matter to you. We'll return to them shortly.

IF MY MIND CAN CONCEIVE IT AND MY HEART CAN BELIEVE IT, THEN I CAN ACHIEVE IT.

MUHAMMAD ALI, BOXER

So now you have a list of limiting beliefs that are, for now at least, true *and* important. There are certain things you know about yourself that have a negative bearing on the kind of cycling you can do.

What to do? Remember, a limiting belief tells you:

— I can't do X, because Y

There are two variables here, and we can tackle them both. We can change the limiting belief, Y, so it's no longer true. Or we can change the limitation, X, so it no longer matters.

THE Y FACTOR

Think back to Josh and the Mallorca 312. He has justified his belief that he's not fit enough to complete it successfully, and he knows it to be true. But could he *get* fit enough? He only has three months, but could he enlist a personal trainer, dedicate a couple of hours a day to Zwift, lose weight, score some performance-enhancing drugs, and do everything else he'd need to do to get himself in shape quickly?

Yes, given time, money, and all the other stuff he'd need to address to make this possible, it is by no means physically impossible for Josh to prepare for the event in 3 months.

Which means Y is now a limiting belief only in terms of logistics. It's no longer a *psychological* barrier. That distinction is so very important. As soon as he understands that it's merely difficult, not impossible, to get in shape in time, Josh can shed his conviction that he can't ride the Mallorca 312. He absolutely could. It would be hard but, in principle, he could find a way.

The reality is that it's just too impractical, and he's not prepared to give up his job and spend all his savings. But that's okay. That's his choice. He still has a limiting belief, but now he can frame it like this:

— I can't ride the Mallorca 312 event this year because I don't have the resources to train sufficiently in the time available.

Logistics all the way.

THE X FACTOR

What if Josh changes X? What if he could find another goal that's just as motivating, but a lot more practical? What if he accepted the situation, but figured out a way of adapting to it? This takes us back to motivation. Josh needs to drill down into why he wants to do the Majorca 312. Why does this challenge in particular mean so much to him?

One possibility is that Josh discovers the Mallorca 312 isn't actually that important to him after all. So often, we find ourselves chasing goals that we haven't really examined. That's why in Part 3, when you find your Mental Cyclist Challenge, you'll be very careful indeed to do just that. Because if you're not fully committed to and motivated by your goals, your *Yeah, But* voice is going to destroy your willpower.

The Mallorca 312 is very clearly a performance goal for most people. Your thinking going into it is going to be more focused on getting through it in one piece in the time available than on the lovely views. Josh might ask himself why it's important to him to complete this gruelling (probably gruesome) event. Is he really driven by performance goals to that extent? Possibly. But possibly not. It's important to know.

Let's say Josh loves cycling in Mallorca. The roads, scenery and weather are all amazing. If that's his primary motivation, he could go to Mallorca and ride the route over 2 or 3 days, in line with his current fitness. He wouldn't do the event, but he would love the cycling. Maybe make it into a touring holiday. Maybe go with some friends.

If he really wants to do the organised event, perhaps because he knows it would be something to be proud of forever, he could do it next year. Register early, design an effective training plan, and have something to look forward to and prepare for properly. Is that so bad?

Or if he really wants a challenge this year, he could park the Mallorca 312 and think about alternative challenges that would be equally memorable but much more achievable right now. Maybe treat this year's challenge as a warm-up for the main event next year.

So let's revisit Josh's revised limiting belief:

— I can't ride the Mallorca 312 event this year, because I don't have the resources to train sufficiently in the time available.

By considering alternatives, he can flip his thinking:

— I can ride the Mallorca 312 route later this year, once I've had time to train.

— I can ride the Mallorca 312 route anytime I choose, taking 2 or 3 days.

— I can ride the organised Mallorca 312 event next year, or any other year.

— I can choose any number of equally challenging events or routes this year, in line with my current fitness and ability to train.

Plenty of options.

Whether you think you can or you think you can't, you're right.
Henry Ford, industrialist

What of Josh's fear of descending? His limiting belief is:

— I can't descend well (Y), because I'm scared of heights (X) and lack the appropriate bike skills (X).

So there are a couple of X factors at play here, and they affect different variations of the Y theme. On a scary road, Josh is terrified he'll fall (or leap?) over the edge and plunge to his death. On a safer descent, he struggles to ride the bends with confidence, which means he goes slowly and doesn't enjoy it. In neither scenario is he a happy cyclist.

GOING DUTCH

This time, let's examine Y first. Is this something Josh can adapt to? Yes, absolutely. He just has to avoid hills. There are plenty of flat rides to enjoy. He could tour the Netherlands or move to Ohio. There are always alternatives.

If Josh decides that avoiding descents forever is impractical, how about the two X factors? Well, fear of heights is a psychological issue that can't simply be cured with a flip of the mind. Perhaps Josh could undertake therapy to tackle it. If that's not an option for him, or until it is, he could (and definitely should) change Y to avoid mountainous rides with perilous cliff–edge descents.

How about the bike skills required to descend safely, quickly and enjoyably? Josh's current lack of confidence is in his head, but those are absolutely skills that he can learn. He could watch YouTube videos and practise carefully and progressively. Or he could work with a coach for a while. He might also get a bike with hydraulic disc brakes that significantly improve braking power and make the business of descending a bit less daunting.

There's plenty he can do to change or sidestep his limiting belief. There always is, if you see your limiting beliefs clearly.

IF THE MIND CAN CAUSE STRESS, THE MIND CAN ALLEVIATE IT. IT'S WITHIN OUR POWER TO CHOOSE ONE THOUGHT OVER ANOTHER, TO CHOOSE OPTIMISM OVER PESSIMISM.

ERNEST CADORIN, AUTHOR

Limiting beliefs have consequences. They tell you that you can't do something because you don't have the right resources. But you don't need limiting beliefs in your cycling. Nobody does. Drilling into them and seeing them for what they are — barriers to having the best possible time on your bike — is hugely liberating.

Revisit your remaining limiting beliefs from the previous exercise and pick one that feels most important right now. You're going to change it from a limiting belief into an achievement goal by considering alternatives to X and fixes for Y. You can change either X or Y, or both. It doesn't matter. What does matter is finding a way to shed this limiting belief and emerge with an exciting new goal.

I CAN'T DO X: **BECAUSE Y:**

....

....

....

What are the alternatives for X?   How can I change Y?

....

....

....

ACHIEVEMENT GOAL

I can do this: By doing this:

....

....

....

— Believing in something isn't the same as knowing it. You know you have legs, but you used to believe in the Tooth Fairy.

— When you question your limiting beliefs, you discover that many of them are untrue. And others don't matter.

— If you face a genuine obstacle rather than a limiting belief, consider alternative goals that you can focus on instead.

NOTES

Looking back over this stage, what have you learned about yourself?

1. ....

....

....

....

2. ....

....

....

....

3. ....

....

....

....

....

THE MENTAL CYCLIST MANIFESTO
STAGE 7

SHAKE
OFF STRESS

Do you know the movie *Falling Down*? William Foster is having the baddest of all bad days. He's wrecked his marriage, he's lost his job, and when he tries to get across the city for his daughter's birthday, he gets caught in a frustrating traffic jam. In the baking heat his air-conditioning fails, and he snaps — he loses his temper, abandons his car in the middle of the motorway, and sets out to make the rest of the journey on foot. It's a bad decision that leads to bad experiences, which in turn lead to some really, really bad decisions.

And a very unhappy ending for all concerned.

THE CAMEL'S BACK

You'll see a very similar journey in lots of other films. The trope of the final straw, of the person under so much pressure that they do or experience bad things, is in all kinds of movies, from the earliest black and white thrillers to 2019's *Joker*. The details and decisions may differ, but the core story is the same: they're stressed, and they get more stressed — and then they snap.

See any parallels with your cycling? Those days when nothing goes right, one problem leads to another, then a car runs over your Oakleys, your wheels fall off, and a sinkhole devours your Pinarello?

Stress in cycling is rubbish. It holds you back, makes you tense and miserable, and sucks the joy out of everything. But here's the secret. Cycling doesn't need to be stressful. The trick is understanding why you suffer stress — and knowing what to do about it.

THE SKY IS NOT FALLING

There are lots of different definitions of stress. We like author Eckhart Tolle's version:

—   Stress is caused by being 'here' but wanting to be 'there.'

The psychological usage of the word (it has different meanings in physics and in speech) is credited to Dr Hans Selye, from 1936. He described stress as:

—   The non-specific response of the body to any demand for change.

Selye found that when animals were exposed to unpleasant stimuli, such as extremes of heat and cold, blaring noises, too-bright light or frustration, they developed health problems. It's a classic case of your mind controlling your body. Stress can make previously healthy people feel unwell, and in some cases can actually make them unwell. As Selye put it:

— It's not stress that kills us. It is our reaction to it.

Stress is your body's reaction to pressure, or perceived pressure. That reaction is not just a single thing; it's a minestrone of negativity, a blend of unpleasant emotions that may include anxiety, anger, frustration and even panic. It can lead you to behave irrationally, to lash out blindly, or to freeze with fear. And it's different for everyone.

Worry is a misuse of the imagination.
Dan Zadra, publisher

Here's a fun exercise for getting a handle on what freaks you out. Make a list of situations in cycling that you find stressful, and score each from 1–5, where 1 is something you can usually shrug off and 5 turns you into William Foster with a bazooka.

Focus on *external* factors here — things that can happen *to* you. There's an important difference between falling off your bike because you hit a patch of ice, which is external, and fear of descending, which is internal. Both are stressful but internal stress factors are best treated as limiting beliefs, as we've just done.

1. .... ☐

2. .... ☐

3. .... ☐

4. .... ☐

5. .... ☐

6. .... ☐

7. .... ☐

8. .... ☐

9. .... ☐

10. .... ☐

One of the best ways of understanding stress is to think of a rollercoaster — one of the good ones, full of people being thrown around at high speed from great heights. If you look at the passengers, some will have raced to the very front of the carriages where they can get the best, most frightening experience. Some will be at the back, visibly anxious and most probably dragged onto the ride by someone else. They clearly don't want to be there and they're not going to enjoy it, not least because there's a good chance they're going to be sick.

The excitable people scream with joy, the scared people with terror. Some people aren't particularly bothered one way or the other, and they don't scream at all.

STRESSED OUT

That's pretty much how stress works. You and I can experience the same stressors — the same events, situations or worries that cause stress — but react completely differently. The reason for that is simple. Stressors do not actually cause stress. They're just things that happen. Those things *induce* stress, certainly, but that's down to us.

Now, hold up, you say. This sounds strange. Possibly plain wrong. Of course stressors cause stress! That's why the first part of the word is "stress". But when you consider what's really going with stress, you'll realise that they don't. Whether or not you feel stress in any situation, whenever anything happens, is entirely within your control. In fact, feeling stress is a choice you make.

That's because what causes stress is your emotional reaction to the situation — the way you *feel* about the situation — not the situation itself. If your emotional reaction is negative, you're going to feel stressed. But if you don't have that reaction, you're not going to experience any of the mental or physical symptoms of stress. You'll be up the front of the rollercoaster, waving your arms in the air. Or handling the ride with detached composure — whichever you prefer. Because you get to choose.

Confidence is the stuff that turns
thoughts into action.
Richard Petty, psychologist

Say you're riding in a sportive, and halfway around you get a puncture. It's an unfortunate situation but there's nothing you can do to avoid it, because it's already happened.

It's quite fair to imagine that your puncture would lead to stress at this point. You might feel frustration, disappointment or even anger. Frustration because you've suddenly encountered an obstacle that's stopped you in your tracks; disappointment because your time is going to suffer and all your buddies are now way down the road; and anger directed at whoever or whatever caused the puncture — the cycling gods, the council workers who cut the hedgerow but didn't clear up the thorns, or yourself because you bought cheap tyres instead of those Kevlar–lined Continentals you really wanted.

Then there's all the stuff you have to do next, which might include:

—   Changing or patching the tube.

—   Fixing a slash in the tyre.

—   Borrowing a tube from another rider because you're all out.

—   Borrowing tyre levers because you've lost your own.

—   Asking another rider for help because you *did* buy Kevlar–lined tyres and now you can't get them off the damn rim.

—   Getting cold, wet, dirty etc.

—   Wrestling with a tiny pump that fits neatly in your pocket but has all the inflation capacity of an asthmatic ant.

—   Immediately puncturing again because you forgot to check the inside of the tyre for anything sharp.

—   Riding hard to try to catch up with your mates.

—   Grinding across an open moor in grumpy solitude because you couldn't.

In a matter of moments, your mood and your motivation have completely changed. You were flying along in a state of flow, and now your bike's upside–down in a puddle and you're inventing expletives.

THE UNIVERSAL

But let's consider this some more. The situation you're experiencing is universal. It doesn't matter who's experiencing it, because a puncture is a puncture. The fact there's a great big thorn sticking out of the rubber while the tyre goes hissssssssssssss is a *fact*, not an opinion.

But that's the *only* objective, universal thing happening here. Everything else, from the way you see the situation, to the way it makes you feel, to the way it affects what you do next, is subjective and personal. You might approach the puncture calmly and fix it without fuss so you can get back in the saddle as quickly as possible. Another rider encountering an identical puncture in identical circumstances might turn the air blue in a spectacle of purple-faced rage before throwing their bike into the newly cut hedge. The situations are identical, but the emotional and behavioural reactions are dramatically different.

Ah, that's all down to personality, we say. Dave's a buddha on the bike, fazed by nothing, while Kate's a fiery hothead, only ever one wee incident away from an explosion. And that's true, in a way, but it's not very helpful. What *would* be helpful is getting to the root of where stress comes from so we can understand it, then blow it up and ride with big smiles on our stress-free faces.

THE MISSING LINK

Here's what you *think* is happening when you experience stress and react accordingly:

SITUATION   >   FEELING   >   REACTION

PUNCTURE   >   STRESS   >   SCREAM AT THE STARS

The way you behave, and how you continue to feel after the situation, is absolutely driven by the way you feel when it happens. But the way you feel when it happens is *not* caused directly by the situation. There's a missing link here, which we so often overlook because it happens automatically and unconsciously. Here's what really happened:

SITUATION   >   PERCEPTION   >   STRESS   >   REACTION

It's your *perception* of the situation that generates the feeling of stress, not the situation itself. How you perceive the situation, which includes how you *interpret* it and how you *judge* it, is what makes you feel good, bad, murderous or suicidal. The way you perceive situations happens unconsciously but it affects everything, so we need to figure out what's going on under the hood.

To do this, we need to talk about binary thinking and value judgements.

BINARY IS FOR COMPUTERS, NOT CYCLISTS

We humans really like to divide the world into two. Black or white. Boy or girl. Rich or poor. Success or failure. Big or small. Mind or body. Fast or furious. Okay, maybe not that last one. But you get the idea. We do it because it makes life easy. It's a shortcut, a way of simplifying stuff that's a lot more complicated.

Which is fine. But then we make it complicated in a different way by bolting on value judgements. This box here is the *good* stuff; this box at the other end of the spectrum is *bad*. We do binary thinking in politics, where Party A are good people and Party B are agents of Satan. We do it in music, where genre P is exciting and genre Q just a bunch of honking sounds. And we do it in cycling, where tailwinds are awesome and headwinds are awful.

In fact, value judgements are particularly common in cycling because we can easily quantify things as positive or negative, success or failure. In races, there's a winner — and then everyone else. In hill climbs there can be target times and personal bests, or even deeply personal targets such as Wiping The Smug Smile Off Lightning Mike's Face or Doing Better Than Bloody Susan. You either hit them or you don't. Succeed or fail.

When the puncture happened, you immediately, subconsciously, made a value judgement. You perceived the puncture as a bad situation. Not just inconvenient or unexpected, but *bad*. It's that loaded perception that causes the stress and ruins your ride.

It turns out that binary is brilliant for computers, but it's pretty rubbish for everything else. Because binary thinking is a trap!

— It's a trap because you're constantly at the mercy of all kinds of factors that affect your emotions, your behaviour, and the consequences of that.

— It's a trap because you'll only feel great if you're a winner and terrible if you fall even slightly short, even if it wasn't your fault.

— It's a trap because it straps you into an emotional rollercoaster that you don't control.

— It's a trap because it means that for every boost there's a barrier, for every success a failure, for every step forwards a pothole to fall into and twist your ankle.

— It's a trap because it keeps you oscillating constantly from extreme to extreme — I'm the best! I'm the worst! It's draining. It saps your energy. It affects your performance and enjoyment, and ruins your cycling.

ROOT OUT YOUR VALUE JUDGEMENTS

We make value judgements all the time. If you look around you right now, you'll probably find something to provoke an emotional response. It could be someone with a grating voice or a drippy sniff. It could be a clickbait newspaper headline. It could be the way time seems to have stopped on the office clock.

Here are some other examples:

— A passenger eating a really pungent egg sandwich on the train.
— A driver cutting you up at the lights.
— A cyclist mounting the pavement and startling pedestrians.

These are all negatives. But there are plenty of positives too:

— A passenger smiling and moving their stuff to make room for you on the train.
— A driver waving you to let you out of a junction in packed traffic.
— A cyclist stopping to check if you need help with a mechanical problem.

Your emotional responses derive from the way you judge the situation. But because the judgement happens automatically, we usually don't appreciate what's going on under the hood. Here's how we judge these situations (or how I do, anyway).

SITUATION	FEELING	JUDGEMENT
A passenger eating a really pungent egg sandwich on the train.	Revulsion.	That passenger has no self-awareness or just doesn't care about other people.
A driver cutting you up at the lights.	Frustration.	That driver has a problem with cyclists or just drives like an arse.
A cyclist mounting the pavement and startling pedestrians.	Anger.	That cyclist is selfish, dangerous, and a bit of a dick.
A passenger smiling and moving their stuff to make room for you on the train.	Grateful.	That passenger is kind-hearted and considerate.
A driver waving you to let you out of a junction in packed traffic.	Appreciative.	That driver is fair and respectful.
A cyclist stopping to check if you need help with a mechanical problem.	Supported.	Cyclists are awesome.

The following exercise will help you lift the lid on your own value judgements.

Value judgements are destructive to our proper business, which is curiosity and awareness.
John Cage, philosopher

This is an exercise in observation and analysis, designed to help you understand where your feelings are coming from.

SITUATION
Think of three recent situations that caused a significant emotional reaction.

1. ....

2. ....

3. ....

FEELING

How did each situation make you feel? Put a name to your emotion and flag it as positive or negative.

	+	−
1.	☐	☐
2.	☐	☐
3.	☐	☐

JUDGEMENT

What value judgement are you making about the situation? This gets to the heart of why you're making a judgement and how that judgement is affecting the way you feel.

....

....

....

....

....

....

....

....

We've looked at what really happens inside your head when a situation affects you:

SITUATION   >   PERCEPTION   >   STRESS   >   REACTION

We're not going to get bogged down in an ethical discussion here, puffing on pipes (or vapes) while pontificating about whether ethical values are part of the very fabric of our existence, or an arbitrary layer we superimpose on our experience as conscious beings in an effort to impose meaning and order on a cold and empty universe that would otherwise drive us howling mad. And I'm not suggesting that you shouldn't have any binary boxes or value judgements in your thinking. Of course you should. Racism, poverty, and drivers who don't give cyclists enough room are all indisputably bad. Properly bad, not 'bad' in scare quotes.

COOL YOUR JETS

But I am suggesting that if you can find a way to handle situations without automatically jumping to built-in emotional reactions and behaviours, you'll enjoy your cycling a whole lot more. If you don't judge a situation to be positive or negative, good or bad, you won't have a positive or negative emotional response. Which means you won't feel stress. And you won't have any negative behavioural reactions either.

Stress has consequences that are often not in your best interest. It's no fun being a slave to your emotions. It's generally calm heads and cool behaviour that win the day, not William Foster with his bazooka blowing up the road in *Falling Down*. When your ship hits an iceberg, it's smarter to find a lifeboat than throw the captain overboard.

But I could show my prowess
Be a lion, not a mow-ess
If I only had the nerve...
Cowardly Lion, Wizard of Oz

It's helpful to think of your mental process in a stress–inducing situation as a chain, partly because it chains you to unhelpful patterns of behaviour, but also because chains can be broken.

I bet you don't often turn to 1980s pop star Howard Jones for life advice, but his chart hit New Song urged everybody to "challenge preconceived ideas", say "goodbye to long-standing fears", and "throw off your mental chains (woo-hoo-hoo)". On Top of The Pops, Jones drove this point home with the subtlety 80s pop stars were famous for. As he played, a sad–faced mime covered in chains made it clear that he'd be a much happier mime if he could only throw off the chains that prevented him from achieving his full potential.

THE WEAKEST LINK

They don't make them like they used to. Anyway, throwing off, or at least breaking, your mental chains is exactly what you need to do here. There are three links in the chain, and we can target them all.

You can change the connection between:

SITUATION > PERCEPTION   How you perceive and judge the situation

PERCEPTION > STRESS   How that perception creates feelings of stress

STRESS > REACTION   How you react to stress

And, of course, you can sometimes also change the situation (although not if the situation has already happened). We'll look at that in Stage 9.

Let's revisit our puncture. It's a stressful — correction: stress–*inducing* — situation, so let's explore what's really happening. We'll work backwards and explore:

—   The behavioural reaction caused by feelings of stress.
—   The feelings of stress caused by the perception of the situation.
—   The perception of the situation caused by unconscious, value–laden binary thinking.

To change the way you react to feelings of stress, you can train yourself to not react like you normally would. You'll still be stressed because you're not doing anything to address that, but you can retrain your brain not to react as it usually does. It's the same principle behind the way we treat phobias; therapy and progressive exposure can get you over your fear of heights, spiders, or clowns.

We use the same tactics to get over the white-knuckled fear that some of us get doing things such as public speaking or performing, or just meeting people when we're shy. You can train yourself not to enter a zone of ruddy-faced rage when you hit a headwind or get a puncture, and learn to accept it with a resigned shrug instead.

As you control your behaviour, you'll find the stress slips away and you can handle the situation calmly.

BREATHE, BREATHE IN THE AIR

When stress hits you, you tend to react pretty quickly. But what if you could find a little space between your feelings and your behaviour? A little breathing space? Just time enough to take Three Mental Breaths and ask yourself three questions about the stress you're feeling.

In psychology, there's a technique known as cognitive reframing. It's based on the work of Aaron T Beck in the 1960s. He found that patients with depression experienced powerfully negative thoughts. By reframing those thoughts, by thinking more positively, their depression lessened. With cognitive reframing, you effectively intercept the negative thoughts and interrogate them.

Whenever you experience stressful feelings, take Three Mental Breaths and ask yourself:

— What just happened?
— How does it affect me?
— What should I do now?

You may be feeling stress because your unconscious value judgement is calling this a 'bad' situation, but here you immediately push back and say:

— Nope, that's not what matters here. What matters is what happens next.

What you're doing is dealing with a situation without immediately feeling negative emotions such as frustration, anger, disappointment, anxiety, spittle-flecked fury, and all the other ingredients in the minestrone soup of stress.

Imagine responding not with a string of F-bombs, but with a more measured:

— Right, that's unfortunate. What's the best way to fix this?

That response is where you need to get to anyway, but it's a lot less stressful if you don't have to wade through a swamp of negative emotions to reach it.

07.07   FOCUS ON YOUR FEELINGS

If you struggle to put a lid on your feelings before they overwhelm you, try this. Acknowledge how you're feeling and take a few more deep breaths. Then ask yourself three questions.

— Is it rational to feel this way?
— Is it helpful to feel this way?
— Is it necessary to feel this way?

Let's look at these in turn.

RATIONAL?

Sometimes it feels perfectly rational to feel stressed. When some clown pulls out in front of you or squeezes past without leaving enough room, then of course you're going to be angry. Your value judgement is that poor driving endangers life, and it's definitely a stretch to react to a near-death experience with a shrug.

But a lot of the time we don't react rationally. We overreact, or we jump to conclusions that may well be wrong, or we let stress factors from other parts of our lives affect our response. For example, if you've had a bad day at work or a row with your partner, then your tolerance for the idiocy of other road users drops dramatically. Things you'd normally dismiss as part and parcel of everyday riding make you absolutely furious. People to whom you'd normally give the benefit of doubt become monsters. Throw in some stress, and suddenly you're blaming Mother Nature herself for the existence of thorns.

So, when stress hits, take those Three Mental Breaths and quickly assess whether you might be over-reacting. Introspection is not always easy to do in the heat of the moment. It can feel a bit like your partner asking whether you're moody today because of your hormones, to which the appropriate and legally acceptable response is a bullet to the head. However, remember that mental cycling is about getting to know yourself. Indulge yourself with those deep, mindful breaths, and assess your feelings calmly. That alone can often help to defuse the stress.

If not, be prepared to accept that yes, it *is* rational to be feeling stressed right now. That's ok.

HELPFUL?

But is it helpful to feel this way? This one is easy. If you feel stressed, the answer is no. Stress isn't helpful unless it's the kind of stress that motivates you, such as a crucial deadline. Stress as a response to an irritating situation isn't that kind of stress.

Being profoundly pissed off or absolutely f—ing furious may be rational and completely understandable, but it's never helpful. It doesn't add any value, it doesn't do anything to help you deal with the situation, and it may well make the situation even worse. The extreme example of that is road rage, when a minor bump can become major fisticuffs. But any kind of anger, frustration, or negativity can impair your ability to assess the situation, work out what to do, and do it.

So, have a word with yourself and note that feeling this way really isn't helpful at all. Then cut yourself some slack and be kind. See if you can mentally reach out to your stressometer and dial it down.

NECESSARY?

Finally, ask yourself whether you have to feel this way. Again, the answer is no. It's not necessary. If you feel stressed and react badly, that's a choice you're making. You can choose to feel otherwise.

Now, some people do the following exercise and have a blinding flash:

—   I don't need to feel this way! I don't need to let my feelings get the better of me!

But for many of us, it's a bit more complicated than that. We understand on an intellectual level that our reactions are based on a complex patterns of perceptions and biases, binary boxes and value judgements (and what someone once said to us in primary school). But then a situation arises and we forget all of that because we're immediately furious, or frustrated, or anxious, or upset.

It's just that we're naturally hot-headed, we'll say. We're easily discouraged. We can't help ourselves. We know it's not rational, we know it's not helpful, but it's just our personality. It's just who we are.

—   It's just who I am.

It's not who you are.

MIND YOUR EMOTIONS

Try seeing the feelings that lead to your behaviour in a different way. We're moving into mindfulness territory here. Mindfulness doesn't differentiate between positive and negative emotions, because they're both unhelpful. Feelings are neither positive nor negative. They're just feelings that you can notice and move on from.

For example, instead of thinking: "I've had a puncture, and I'm really annoyed because my performance target is toast", you can observe: "I notice feelings of annoyance within myself". It's a subtle difference, but it's an important one. The first version says:

— I am a thing: annoyed!

The second says:

— I notice a thing: a feeling of annoyance within me.

We notice all kinds of things all the time. Then we let them pass by, and we get on with what we're doing. Feelings of annoyance, or of anger, or of anything else, don't have to affect you if you don't let them.

Our reaction to self-criticism is more important than the self-criticism itself. Paying attention to our reactions is very important because the only thing we have control over is how we react.
Yong Kang Chan, mindfulness teacher

We're right back at the source of your feelings: your perception of the situation, powered by your value judgements. Can you change this?

The truth is that most situations don't require or deserve value judgements. These judgements are entirely superfluous. Rain isn't good or bad; it's just a weather condition, and how it affects you depends largely on how well prepared you are for it. A climb isn't easy or hard; it's just a gradient in the road that has implications for your physical effort and mental focus at this moment. Strava stats are just a measure of performance, not tokens of good and evil.

And a puncture's just a puncture.

CHOOSE SMART

When you allow value judgements to shape your feelings and cause you stress, that's a choice you make. Yes, a choice made on autopilot based on years of accumulated attitudes and experience, but it's still a choice. Value judgements are not hard-wired into your brain, and that means you can choose not to make them.

There's a very famous speech by the late writer David Foster Wallace called *This Is Water*. In it, he talks about a typical experience of going shopping after a hard day at work. You have to fight through rush-hour traffic, the supermarket sound system is playing music you hate, the aisles are crowded — and everybody in the shop is an idiot.

As he puts it:

—   Who are all these people in my way? And look at how repulsive most of them are, and how stupid and cow-like and dead-eyed and nonhuman they seem in the checkout line, or at how annoying and rude it is that people are talking loudly on cell phones in the middle of the line. And look at how deeply and personally unfair this is.

In Wallace's examples, we immediately make the most negative value judgements. That makes us feel frustrated, and irritable, and maybe even angry. But if we made different value judgements, we'd feel completely different emotions. As Wallace writes:

—   But most days, if you're aware enough to give yourself a choice, you can choose to look differently at this fat, dead-eyed, over-made-up lady who just screamed at her kid in the checkout line. Maybe she's not usually like this. Maybe she's been up three straight nights holding the hand of a husband who is dying of bone cancer. Or maybe this very lady is the low-wage clerk at the motor vehicle department, who just yesterday helped your spouse resolve a horrific, infuriating, red-tape problem through some small act of bureaucratic kindness.

Of course, none of this is likely, but it's also not impossible. The truth is, you just don't know. So why roll with the negative?

YOU CHOOSE YOU

You can choose to make alternative, positive value judgements. To think the best rather than the worst. Or you can choose not to apply value judgements at all. This allows you to regard every situation neutrally. When you do that — when you *choose* to do that — you won't feel stress.

This is not the same as forcing yourself not to react as you normally would to a stressful situation. And it's not the same as analysing your feelings of stress and trying to defuse negativity with logic and pragmatism. It's about switching off the automatic value judgement tap so you don't see situations as good or bad.

We are our choices.
Jean-Paul Sartre, philosopher

VALUE JUDGEMENTS CONCERNING LIFE, FOR OR AGAINST, CAN IN THE LAST RESORT NEVER BE TRUE: THEY POSSESS VALUE ONLY AS SYMPTOMS... IN THEMSELVES SUCH JUDGEMENTS ARE STUPIDITIES.

FRIEDRICH NIETZSCHE, PHILOSOPHER

We've just looked at several strategies for dealing with stress on a bicycle. This exercise is all about reflection, imagination, and practice. First, reflect on a stressful situation when you reacted in a way that wasn't particularly helpful, like our old friend William Foster in *Falling Down*. Then imagine behaving differently in that exact same situation.

Next time you encounter a stress-inducing situation on your bike, take your Three Mental Breaths and put a little (breathing) space between yourself and what's just happened. Think about this exercise and imagine how you could react differently to normal.

SITUATION
What happened?

REACTION

How did you react when it happened? Just the facts here, including any consequences.

FEELING

How did you feel when it happened? Again, just the facts.

PERCEPTION

How did you judge the situation when it happened? Think beyond your feelings and reaction, and get to the heart of why it made you feel and behave as it did.

ALTERNATIVE REACTION

How could you have reacted differently? Can you imagine not being a slave to your emotions?

ALTERNATIVE FEELING

Could you have felt differently? What would have been more rational and helpful?

ALTERNATIVE PERCEPTION

How could you have perceived and judged the situation differently, so you didn't feel and behave the way you did?

— Stress sucks the joy out of things, but it's not inevitable and you aren't powerless against it. It's our emotional response to stressful things that matters.

— The only fact is what you're dealing with right now. Everything else — your interpretation of the situation, how it makes you feel, what you decide to do — is up to you.

— Binary is brilliant for computers and terrible for cyclists. Avoid thinking in terms of good vs bad, success vs failure, triumph vs disaster.

— You can retrain yourself to react in different ways to potential stressors.

NOTES

Looking back over this stage, what have you learned about yourself?

1. _____

_____

_____

_____

2. _____

_____

_____

_____

3. _____

_____

_____

_____

THE MENTAL CYCLIST MANIFESTO

STAGE 8

THWART
THE THREATS

How do you feel when you're under pressure? Pumped full of adrenaline, your superhero cape at the ready, an unstoppable force of willpower and unshakeable self-belief? Or would you rather hide under a blanket and hope it goes away?

If you're closer to the latter, chances are you're interpreting *challenges* as *threats*. The distinction is important. A challenge is something you can overcome, like training a wayward puppy. A threat is something to avoid, like an angry bear. If you react to an angry bear as you would to a puppy, you'll soon find yourself in trouble. But if you react to puppies as if they were angry bears, you'll undermine your abilities and limit your options.

PRESSURE VALVE

We've all heard the management nonsense (and John Lennon lyric) about how there are no problems, only solutions. No threats, only challenges. But like many clichés, there's a grain of truth to it. How we approach a situation, and the language we use to describe it, even in our own heads, has a direct effect on how we feel. The glass-half-full person will typically be more positive and proactive than the glass-half-empty one. Thinking about your puppy like this:

—   It's impossible — she just won't stop peeing on the carpet!

Is the same territory as thinking like this on your bike:

—   It's too hard, too high, too windy — I just can't do this!

The impact goes far beyond your immediate mood. In the bigger picture, in life and on the bike, the way you frame things in your mind affects your ability to do what you want and/ or need to do.

And that affects everything.

We all know someone who's good under pressure. When a decision needs to be made, they make it. People who are good under pressure are not necessarily smarter or more capable than others. But what they can do is park their negative emotions so they don't get in the way of what needs to be done. They can separate themselves from the situation and look at it calmly and objectively. It's an important skill.

More is lost by indecision than wrong decision.
Tony Soprano, mobster

People who are not so good under pressure – or at least, people who don't consider themselves to be good under pressure – are less likely to do that. Instead, they'll experience the physical symptoms of stress. If the pressure is extreme, they may feel fear and even panic. Those negative feelings prevent them from focusing, from making decisions, and ultimately from doing anything at all.

Inaction seldom ends well. Rabbit, headlights, roadkill.

08.02   YOU'VE GOT TO HAVE FAITH

If you see something as a challenge, that's a positive mindset. Mentally, you frame the situation as something you can deal with. It might be hard or complicated, but it's probably doable. However, if you see it as a threat, that's a negative mindset. You're likely to get stressed and anxious, which will set you up for failure.

The people with clipboards call it TCTSA – the Theory of Challenge and Threat States in Athletes. That's theory in the scientific sense of something you collate evidence to demonstrate, not in the internet forum sense of "something I just pulled out of my backside".

We're going to simplify it a bit because if we didn't, we'd be banging on for ages. But the gist is really straightforward. There are three key things to consider.

1. YOUR ABILITY TO SUCCEED IS DIRECTLY AFFECTED BY YOUR BELIEF IN YOUR ABILITY TO SUCCEED

Completing a task requires resources: your time, your energy, your skills, and so on. If you have the resources to complete the task, it's a challenge. If you don't, it's a threat. So you always need to ask:

—   Do I believe I have the resources for this?

You may feel that your resources are definitely up to the task. It might be an easy challenge, like a short training run. No stress, you can do it no problem. Or it may be a tougher situation, like running on empty with 15 miles to go and wishing you were anywhere but in the saddle. So long as you know you can make it home without keeling over, you're in a challenge state. You might not be happy about it, but you won't be anxious.

However, if things go really wrong and you don't believe you have the resources required, what happens then? Turns out you have choices:

—   Quit.
—   Press on as best you can.
—   Increase your resources.

Quitting may or may not be an option. Quite often in cycling, there's simply no way to quit. Pressing on might mean pushing for a bit rather than riding. Increasing your resources can mean resting up for a while or taking on some food or latching onto a group and sheltering in the wheels. Whatever options are open to you are worth grabbing. But if you have no options, you'll wish you'd never started. It's not a happy headspace to be in. Threat states are grim.

—   I have to do this!
—   I can't do this!
—   But I have to!
—   But I really, really can't!
—   Bugger.

However, there is an alternative. You can change your belief. If you flip your thinking and convince yourself that you can do it, you'll be in a much better headspace to continue.

Now, a wee warning word about positive thinking. Sometimes, as a matter of fact, not belief, you simply don't have resources available. And you might *know* you don't have the resources. Remember what we discussed earlier about knowledge being justified true belief?

—   There's sound evidence for it. Perhaps your legs are shaking, you can barely lift your head, and you feel more dead than alive.

—   It's true. For example, you're definitely bonking and you have no access to fresh fuel to power your body.

—   You believe it. Maybe you've never been more certain of anything in your life!

Positive thinking will not magic impossible resources out of thin air. Willpower can't win a war when it has no weapons to fight with.

However, some of the time — generally a lot more of the time than we acknowledge — we're not really up against the wall. We just feel we are. So prodding your brain to accept that you could physically do more if your mind says yes rather than *no* can pay dividends. The extent to which you're prepared to do this — to push yourself — is entirely down to you.

If you are motivated by exerting extreme effort, if you have it within yourself to push that extra bit beyond what's usually tolerable, if you're ok entering the pain cave for a while — then acknowledge this about yourself. It's an asset that will serve you well when things get really testy. When the chips are down, turn on your positive thinking and tell yourself — as a matter of fact, not opinion — that you *can* do this thing. Mantras and positive affirmations might help.

But if that's *not* you, be cool with it. Relax and be kind to yourself. Nobody, not even your spin instructor, can make you go further than you're prepared to go. It's absolutely fine to acknowledge that you're not the kind of person who sees suffering in cycling as a positive. It's not a weakness — it's simply what works for you. You probably care more for fun than performance, and what's wrong with that?

2. CONTROL AFFECTS WHETHER YOU ENTER A CHALLENGE STATE OR A THREAT STATE

The more control you have over things you *can* control, like preparing for an event or having options to hand during it, the better you can cope with things you *can't* control, such as somebody else's performance, mechanical issues, weather conditions, oil on the road, and so on.

For every cyclist, there are things you can control and things you cannot. We'll explore that further in the next chapter.

For now, consider that there are two things you can *always* control. These are your attitude and your effort. They are both entirely within your control because they are internal mental factors, not practical or physical stuff that affects you from the outside.

3. IT'S BETTER TO STRIVE TO ACHIEVE SOMETHING THAN TO AVOID SOMETHING

Athletes who are focused on a specific goal do better than those whose plan begins and ends with "try not to lose". Achievement goals — things you can gain, things that matter to you, things you find rewarding, meaningful and enjoyable — are perfect for a challenge state. Whereas avoidance strategies — don't fall off, don't get dropped, don't have a miserable time — are a one-way ticket to Threat State Central.

It's a subtle shift, but an important one. Keeping your eye on achievement goals is a *lot* more motivating than merely trying to avoid disaster. Let's say you're on a diet and currently a size 14. You'd love to slip into those lovely size 12 jeans you bought years ago and haven't worn since. And you really don't want to get larger and have to buy the next size up. Which is more motivating and better for your self-esteem — shooting for size 12 so you feel great in your jeans, or trying to avoid size 16 so you don't feel crap? Achievement goals all the way!

There's a mass of evidence that pushing beyond your comfort zone improves your mental and physical performance. There's even a law about it — the Yerkes–Dodson Law, named after a pair of early 20th Century psychologists. After what seems like a rather excessive amount of time delivering electric shocks to dancing mice, they found that a certain amount of stimulation — in this case, the very natural fear of getting another electric shock — had a noticeable positive effect on the mice's performance as dancers.

IN THE ZONE

There's a very important 'but' to that. The psychologists found that the stimulation only worked up to a point. If the stimulus was too high or went on for too long, it created too much anxiety — and the performance gains were reversed. What applies to traumatised mice applies to us too. If a challenge is beyond your comfort zone *to just the right extent but not too much*, it can drive you to perform better. It's the region where you're still within the limits of your ability to meet the challenge, but only just. Any further out there and you'd be in a threat state — which is where the wild things are. Like angry bears.

Your mental cycling zone is towards the very outer edge of your challenge zone. That's a brilliant place to be.

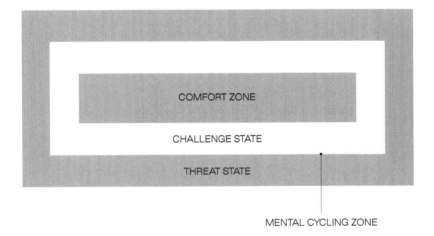

A GOAL SHOULD SCARE YOU A LITTLE AND EXCITE YOU A LOT.

JOE VITALE, AUTHOR

For this exercise, start by recalling an enjoyable ride where you were well within your comfort zone. Remember how you felt during the ride. Next, think about a very different ride when you'd definitely bitten off more than you could chew. Perhaps you found yourself bonking halfway up a hill. Perhaps you felt deep existential terror as you realised you were hopelessly lost in a strange land, with night closing in fast and an angry bear stalking you in the shadows. Again, focus on your feelings at the time. Finally, think about a ride where you were well outside your comfort zone, but believed — most of the time, at least — that you could do this thing.

COMFORT RIDE

....

....

....

I FELT:

....

....

....

....

....

THREAT STATE RIDE

I FELT:

CHALLENGE STATE RIDE

I FELT:

— A challenge is something you can overcome, like training a puppy. A threat is something you can't, like an angry bear. It's important not to confuse the two.

— Positive thinking can push you forwards, so long as it's not just wishful thinking.

— Achievement goals are much more motivating than avoidance goals.

— Pushing beyond your comfort zone improves mental and physical performance, provided the challenge is not too difficult.

NOTES

Looking back over this stage, what have you learned about yourself?

1. ....

....

....

....

2. ....

....

....

....

....

3. ....

....

....

....

....

THE MENTAL CYCLIST MANIFESTO

STAGE 9

DESIGN
YOUR DEFENCES

09.01   CH-CH-CH-CH-CHANGES

You know the cheesy old Serenity Prayer?

> *God, grant me the serenity to accept the things I cannot change,*
> *Courage to change the things I can,*
> *And wisdom to know the difference.*

A stress–inducing cycling situation is something you can change. Lots of stuff can go wrong on a ride. Some of it is completely unpredictable, but the overwhelming majority of stuff that could go wrong can be predicted. If you can predict it, you can mitigate against it. If you do that, you'll be a lot more confident.

What you need is an if/then strategy:

BIT IFFY

We do it all the time. If you believe your performance or enjoyment — or both — are being hindered because you have a rubbish bike, then getting a less rubbish bike will solve that particular problem. If your brain's response is to say, "I can't afford a better bike", then you might consider what other things you could sell to help finance it: the guitar you haven't played for a decade, whichever of your children is most annoying, and so on.

—   If I want a new bike, then I can do this to get the money...

There's your strategy.

Sometimes we get hung up on things that are quite easily fixed, in principle at least. For most of us, "I don't have time to train" means "I haven't made the time to train". Similarly, "It's too cold to ride" means "I haven't got the right winter clothes". These things are simple to address with a bit of forward planning and online shopping.

If you're anxious about mechanical problems leaving you stranded miles from home, you might take a course in bicycle maintenance. Now you'll know what to do when things go wrong — and you can carry all the tools and spares you could conceivably need, from spare tubes to a chain splitter and replacement cables. If you're worried about the weather turning wet, you could carry a waterproof. If you're worried about getting lost, you could pre-load maps and routes onto your bike computer. There's no predictable scenario that you can't prepare for.

The trick is thinking ahead and preparing for situations that *could* happen and *would* definitely cause you stress. Which, of course, we don't always do. But definitely should.

WHAT COULD POSSIBLY GO WRONG?

Here are some situations that can catch out cyclists. Check the ones you've already encountered. I've encountered them all at one time or another. If you haven't encountered any, you should think about bottling that good luck and selling it.

— Puncture
— Pump failure
— Snapped chain
— Split tyre
— Flat battery — electronic shifting
— Flat battery — lights
— Broken cleat
— Broken pedal
— Broken spoke(s)
— Snapped brake or gear cable
— Bonking (running out of energy)
— Unexpected weather
— Unexpected darkness
— Computer failure
— Snapped seat post bolt
— Swallowing a fly
— Wasp in your helmet
— Rotted spare tube

Ah, I could go on and on. Cycling's awesome but cycling can be awful. It's smart to get strategic.

I don't believe in pressure. The pressure is not
being prepared for what you want to do.
Colin Kaepernick, civil rights activist

Some of us don't worry at all about what might happen. That's fine until it does happen — at which point a complacent shrug doesn't really cut it.

But many of us worry too much, and that can be a problem. Feeling anxious about stuff that hasn't happened yet is like experiencing stress in advance. And it's definitely possible to take it too far. As Winston Churchill put it:

— When I look back on all these worries, I remember the story of the old man who said on his deathbed that he had had a lot of trouble in his life, most of which had never happened.

COMPLETE CONTROL

It's easy to conclude that the best way to avoid a negative outcome is to avoid any possibility of a negative outcome. After all, you can't lose a race you don't enter or a game you don't play. But by avoiding any possible negative you're also avoiding any possible positive. You can't win a race you don't enter, experience the endorphin run of a ride you didn't make, enjoy an experience you didn't experience.

But here's the thing. You only feel anxious about things you can't control. If you can control them, there's no need to be anxious. It's a bit like willpower, as we discussed earlier. You only need willpower to do something you don't want to do. You only feel anxious when you feel powerless to control the situation.

How about you decide to stop feeling anxiety and adopt a change strategy instead? Plan and prepare rather than hope and panic?

ALWAYS WATCH WHERE YOU ARE GOING. OTHERWISE YOU MAY STEP ON A PIECE OF FOREST THAT WAS LEFT OUT BY MISTAKE.

WINNIE-THE-POOH, BEAR

This is one time when it really pays to don the catastrophic thinking cap and indulge the most paranoid recesses of your imagination. It will pay off, I promise. One day, something really annoying and unpredictable will happens — but you'll find yourself fully in control of the situation because you'd planned for (nearly) every eventuality.

Complete a thorough risk assessment for your next ride. For example, what would you do if your chain snapped? It's not very likely, I know, but it's *possible*. Could you fix it so you can continue? You may find that you make some permanent changes to your kit as a result of this exercise, such as packing a chain breaker tool and a quick link in your saddle bag. Or what would happen if the route is unfamiliar to you and your bike computer broke? What if this happened in an area of poor mobile reception? Perhaps you'd be smart to download an offline map of the area to your phone. But what if your phone ran flat?

So, imagine what *could* happen, how it would affect you, how you would recover from that, and — crucially — what you could do now to mitigate the risks and/or improve your control over the situation should it happen.

CATEGORY: ACCIDENT OR ILLNESS

Situation

Impact

Recovery

Action

CATEGORY: MECHANICAL PROBLEMS

Situation

Impact

Recovery

Action

CATEGORY: LOGISTICS OR WEATHER

Situation

Impact

Recovery

Action

09.03 MIND CONTROL

I said earlier that there are two things you can always control: your attitude and your effort. What does that mean in practice?

Effort is easy. You can push hard or take it easy. Absorb pain or avoid it. Keep going until you hit your targets, come hell or high water, or sit up in the saddle and take a breather. What's really important is acknowledging that your effort is entirely under your own control. You don't have a race director screaming orders in your earpiece to go full gas, into the red — or if you do, you can choose to rip that earpiece right out and enjoy the relaxing sound of tyres on tarmac instead.

Exercising control over your effort is something you can do at the beginning of a ride or training session, and it's smart to do so. Decide how hard or easy you're going to take it today, make that a goal, and stick to it if you can. But, of course, you can also flex your effort during a ride, and what's wrong with that? Feeling strong and up for taking on a segment? Go for it. Feeling a little flat and weary? Take it easy.

You're a Mental Cyclist. Effort comes from your mind, not your legs. Do whatever feels right in the moment.

ALL IN THE ATTITUDE

What about controlling your attitude? Personally, I've always found this a struggle. I have no problem easing up on effort, but I do find it difficult to change my attitude mid-ride, from: "This is hellish. I wish I was dead" to: "What a wonderful privilege to be out on my bike in a blizzard".

What works for me is thinking about my attitude in advance and making a firm commitment to stick with it, no matter what. I don't allow myself any attitudinal flex during the ride. Your mileage may vary but when I set off with a head full of good thoughts and gratitude, nothing shakes it.

Attitude is often described as the little thing that makes a big difference. It truly does. But I don't just mean: adopt a 'positive mental attitude' and everything will be hunky dory. That's way too vague to be helpful. What *is* helpful is understanding the various components of attitude and selecting the bits that suit you best. Cut your coat to fit your cloth. It will definitely be a challenge committing to a cheery disposition on your bike if you're generally a morose kind of creature, so don't do that. 'Determined' may be a better attitude for you than 'cheery'.

So — *choose* your effort, and *design* your attitude. Let's do that now.

IF YOU DON'T LIKE SOMETHING, CHANGE IT. IF YOU CAN'T CHANGE IT, CHANGE YOUR ATTITUDE.

MAYA ANGELOU, POET

Attitude is an adjective. Or rather, a collection of *applied* adjectives. On these pages, we have a big list of positive adjectives. For your next three rides, I invite you to select a set of three adjectives and make this your attitude *du jour*. But don't just check the boxes. Take your Three Mental Breaths and visualise yourself embodying each attitude on your ride, come what may. It only takes a minute for each one, but that minute will repay itself massively on the ride if you find yourself in a stressful situation.

	Ride 1	2	3
Adaptable	☐	☐	☐
Adventurous	☐	☐	☐
Ambitious	☐	☐	☐
Brave	☐	☐	☐
Calm	☐	☐	☐
Careful	☐	☐	☐
Cheery	☐	☐	☐
Considerate	☐	☐	☐
Creative	☐	☐	☐
Decisive	☐	☐	☐
Determined	☐	☐	☐
Dynamic	☐	☐	☐
Easy-going	☐	☐	☐
Energetic	☐	☐	☐
Enthusiastic	☐	☐	☐
Exuberant	☐	☐	☐
Fair-minded	☐	☐	☐
Fearless	☐	☐	☐
Forceful	☐	☐	☐
Friendly	☐	☐	☐
Generous	☐	☐	☐
Helpful	☐	☐	☐

Imaginative	☐	☐	☐
Independent	☐	☐	☐
Intelligent	☐	☐	☐
Inventive	☐	☐	☐
Kind	☐	☐	☐
Optimistic	☐	☐	☐
Passionate	☐	☐	☐
Patient	☐	☐	☐
Persistent	☐	☐	☐
Philosophical	☐	☐	☐
Powerful	☐	☐	☐
Practical	☐	☐	☐
Pragmatic	☐	☐	☐
Pro-active	☐	☐	☐
Quick-witted	☐	☐	☐
Rational	☐	☐	☐
Reliable	☐	☐	☐
Resourceful	☐	☐	☐
Self-confident	☐	☐	☐
Self-disciplined	☐	☐	☐
Sensible	☐	☐	☐
Sociable	☐	☐	☐
Thoughtful	☐	☐	☐
Tough	☐	☐	☐
Versatile	☐	☐	☐
	☐	☐	☐
	☐	☐	☐
	☐	☐	☐

— Worrying too much means you never leave the house. Don't do that.
— Swap anxiety for strategy.
— Choose your effort, design your attitude.

NOTES

Looking back over this stage, what have you learned about yourself?

1. ....

....

....

....

2. ....

....

....

....

3. ....

....

....

....

SOMETIMES WHEN PEOPLE ARE UNDER STRESS, THEY HATE TO THINK, AND IT'S THE TIME WHEN THEY MOST NEED TO THINK.

BILL CLINTON, AUTHOR

THE MENTAL CYCLIST MANIFESTO
STAGE 10

FIND
YOUR FLOW

At a few points in this book, I've invited you to explore a more mindful way of considering your thinking. I asked you to observe the willpower wars dispassionately when your *Yeah, But* voice tries to body-swerve things you should be doing, and again when your *Cruel Critic* tells you how hopeless and worthless you are. When you become an observer of the stuff going on inside your head, rather than an active participant, you are no longer defined and driven by your passing thoughts and feelings. It's a really powerful way of getting clarity and looking at things differently.

In this stage of The Mental Cyclist, we're going to continue the mindfulness theme in a broader way.

THE HERE AND NOW

That's because mental cycling is about being in the moment. If your mind is somewhere else — if it's focusing on the destination, or on a time target, or on anything else other than what's happening right now — then you can't have a meaningful, enjoyable experience. But when you ride mindfully, *every* ride can be meaningful and enjoyable.

Even when it's really tough out there on the road. Remember, you've binned binary thinking. Discomfort or even pain isn't 'bad'; it's just something that you're feeling at this particular moment. Something you've noticed in much the same way that you notice when the wind is cold or the road surface is uneven.

We can't control the future, but we can control the moment. We can control how we process the things that we notice, and how we feel about those things. The more you practice mindfulness, the more automatic it becomes. The more you learn to focus on the moment and not the future, the more you'll experience that moment, and *enjoy* that experience.

It's time to let go of outcomes completely, and switch your focus and feelings to the moment instead.

The little things? The little moments?
They aren't little.
Jon Kabat-Zinn, Stress Reduction Clinic

As cyclists, we're often hyper-focused on outcomes. We'll climb that hill in this time. We'll do so many kilometres today. We'll smash every Strava segment, and share the awesome with everyone we know. There's nothing wrong with targets. But there can be a lot wrong with how we *think* about them. There are four big problems with focusing too strongly on outcomes.

TARGETS DON'T REALLY MATTER

Unless you're a pro who does miles for money, your livelihood isn't on the line here — and your self-esteem definitely shouldn't be either. Outcomes don't really matter. I know that's a challenging, counter-intuitive concept for some of you, but take those Three Mental Breaths and repeat after me:

—　　THEY. DON'T. REALLY. MATTER.

That's not to say you don't want to *achieve* on your bike, whether it's climbing that hill, or completing that distance, or hitting a new personal best. This whole book is about helping you achieve your goals, including your amazing Mental Cyclist Challenge. But it's crucial to understand and accept that individual outcomes don't matter. Whether you succeed or fail doesn't define you and shouldn't affect how you feel about yourself or your cycling.

TARGETS SUCK THE JOY OUT OF EVERYTHING

When you're emotionally attached to an outcome, you can't relax. You get stressed, anxious, and irritable. You try too hard. You beat yourself up. You waste energy that could be used much more productively. And ultimately, you don't enjoy any of it. Who has time for fun when there's so much at stake?

But you're the one setting the stakes in the first place. You're the one pulling targets out of thin air and deciding that if you don't hit them, the universe is against you.

My partner Audrey is, amongst other things, a yoga teacher. She was frustrated by my stubborn refusal to stretch — I'm about as flexible as a rusty Dalek — and wanted to fix me. At the same time, I was helping Audrey push her road cycling from relative newbie to confident sportive rider. So we set ourselves a six-month challenge. Audrey would get me to touch my toes, and I would get her to the top of Mont Ventoux. I still can't touch my toes, though I am a convert to yoga, but Audrey *did* climb the mountain. *How* she did it was pure mental cycling. Here's Audrey in her own words:

❝ *I knew it would be tough. But I was confident I could do it. I'd done my research and sorted my training plan. I rode a lot alone and with Kyle, and even got used to him incessantly calling out the gradients every time the road went up.*

"Is Ventoux as steep as this?" I'd gasp.

"Bit steeper," he'd laugh. "And a lot longer."

But then shit happened. I got sick. And my training plan went out the window.

By the time I got to Provence, I was pretty stressed and anxious. It had been over six weeks since I'd been on a bike. Physically, I wasn't in great shape. My legs alone were not going to get me up that hill. That's when my mind kicked in. I had to think about this ride in a different way.

I had to change my goal — from reaching the top to just going for a ride in the glorious Provençal sunshine. If I got to the top, great. And if I didn't, well... so what? We were here and we could still have fun. My preparations had been scuppered, but nobody died.

As soon as I had this change of mindset, the pressure lifted. I'd been dreading setting out on that ride. Now, I couldn't wait to get going.

Ventoux lived up to the hype. Every pedal stroke took 100% effort. But because I was focused on the journey — and not the outcome — I had one of my best days on a bike ever.

I did make it to the top. In pretty good time, too. And with a great big smile on my face.

A key factor in becoming a Mental Cyclist is losing your emotional attachment to outcomes. This emotional attachment is sometimes called grasping. It's what keeps us oscillating on the pendulum of extremes, forever grasping for the highs, and trying to avoid the lows. If you can change the way you think about outcomes, you'll begin to find your enjoyment of cycling lies in the journey, not whether or not you achieve a particular target.

TARGETS DON'T STOP BAD THINGS FROM HAPPENING

You can control lots of stuff on your bike, but ultimately you can't control the world around you. All kinds of things can affect whether or not you can achieve an outcome you've set. You could have an unfixable mechanical problem or an accident. The people setting the pace may be supercharged with Strava targets or horribly hungover. It could be too hot, too cold, too windy. You could unexpectedly encounter sheep, rocks, diesel spills, or a zombie apocalypse.

We've already looked at if/then planning, and very sensible it is, too. But no amount of contingency planning can completely stop shit from happening. The shit that happens may be different shit to the shit you imagined happening, or it might be the same shit but much shittier, or shittier in an unexpected way. Or you might have avoided something where you expected shit to happen, only for different shit to happen somewhere else. When that happens, if you're deeply attached to some outcomes, you'll feel shit. Which is another word for stressed. And we definitely don't want that.

Bottom line: you have to expect the unexpected and be okay with it.

Every endeavour pursued with passion produces
a successful outcome regardless of the result.
Nick Bollettieri, coach

TARGETS SHOVE YOU INTO BINARY BOXES

Focusing on outcomes encourages binary thinking. There can only be two results — you either do it or you don't. Win or lose.

Let's say you set out to hit a target on your bike. You want to climb that hill without stopping, smash your personal best, ride at a really high average speed, or whatever it is that matters to you today. Binary thinking says there are only two possible outcomes — success or failure. But these are *loaded* terms. They come with value judgements. Success is a *good* thing, and failure is *bad*. The more you care about it, the better and worse success and failure become.

These judgements have emotional consequences. They generate feelings. Success makes you feel great, at least for a while. More of that please! Failure makes you feel rubbish, usually for much longer.

And it doesn't stop there, because the way you feel has an impact on your behaviour and performance. Failing to hit a target might mean that you don't enjoy the rest of your ride, which is a pity. Or it might mean that you shelve future plans to do something amazing because now you don't believe you're up to it. And that's tragic.

NON-ATTACHMENT TO OUTCOMES

Binary thinking encourages us to become even more emotionally invested in outcomes. Sure, you might try to think in shades of grey between black and white, and console yourself that OK, you didn't hit your goal this time but hey, you gained valuable experience, or did a bit better than the last time, or enjoyed it all the same.

But deep down in in your cycling soul, you feel that you failed.

Wouldn't it be better to find a place of relative contentment and ease, free from binary boxes, where outcomes don't matter nearly as much as we think they do? Where you can enjoy — love! — the ride for what it is, rather than where it takes you?

I DEFINE ANXIETY AS EXPERIENCING FAILURE IN ADVANCE.

SETH GODIN, AUTHOR

Set yourself a challenge to ride without a computer or a destination in mind. No stats, no Strava. No measure of success or failure. Not even the *concept* of success or failure.

What's it like? How do you feel? How is it different from your usual rides? Then repeat three more times and each time capture your feelings here.

RIDE 1

DESCRIPTION

FEELINGS

RIDE 2

DESCRIPTION

FEELINGS

RIDE 3

DESCRIPTION

FEELINGS

RIDE 4

DESCRIPTION

FEELINGS

What we're aiming for is something you've almost certainly experienced before. It's called flow. Have you ever been so involved in doing something enjoyable that you've completely lost track of time? If so, you've been in a flow state.

There are lots of different terms for flow, such as being in the zone or being in the groove, but they all mean the same thing. You're in a flow state when you're fully immersed in the moment and completely absorbed in an activity. An activity that's intrinsically enjoyable.

According to Mark de Rond, Professor of Organisational Ethnography at Cambridge University:

—   Flow is said to lift experience from the ordinary to the optimal, to a zen–like state, and it's in precisely those moments that we feel truly alive and in tune with what we are doing.

Isn't that lovely? Truly alive and in tune with what we are doing.

IMMERSION

The term 'flow' was coined by psychologist and Scrabble high score Mihaly Csikszentmihalyi in his influential 1990 book, *Flow — The Psychology of Optimal Experience*. Csikszentmihalyi had spent four decades studying a huge range of people, including musicians, athletes, poets, and chess players to discover what it was that made them spend so much time so fully immersed in their passions. The answer turned out to be what he dubbed 'flow'.

As Csikszentmihalyi later explained in an interview with Wired magazine, flow is:

—   Being completely involved in an activity for its own sake. The ego falls away. Time flies. Every action, movement, and thought follows inevitably from the previous one, like playing jazz. Your whole being is involved, and you're using your skills to the utmost.

The skills bit is important here. You only enter a flow state when the challenge of the task at hand and your skills are well matched. Flow is not the same thing as relaxation. You experience flow when you're riding your bike, not soaking your muscles in a hot bath afterwards.

IN THE GROOVE

Flow is about finding the right balance between the thing you're doing and your ability to do it. If what you're doing is challenging and interesting enough, you can enter into a flow state. But if it's *too* challenging — which takes you into threat state territory — or if it isn't interesting, you won't.

Let's take the example of playing a musical instrument. If you're trying to play a tune, but you have to stop every time there's a chord change because you don't know where to put your fingers yet, you're not going to get into the groove. Conversely, if the tune you're playing is something really easy and repetitive — the riff from The Rolling Stones' *Satisfaction*, perhaps — you're going to get very bored with it very quickly.

It's the same with cycling. We've all experienced flow states on our bikes, but the circumstances in which you achieve that state constantly evolve. Your first two-wheeled flow state probably took place shortly after you took off the stabilisers. These days you need a bit more of a challenge before body and bike come together in perfect harmony.
But when they do, the results are exceptional.

If your skills and the challenge are well matched, you'll experience flow — not just mentally, but physically too. For example, in a 2004 study of classical pianists, *The Psychophysiology of Flow During Piano Playing*, researchers reported that:

—   A significant relation was found between flow and heart period, blood pressure, heart rate variability, activity of the zygomaticus major muscle, and respiratory depth.

The zygomaticus major muscle is the one that makes us smile.

In his studies of flow, Csikszentmihalyi has been particularly fascinated by the characteristic of intrinsic motivation. He found that people who experience intrinsic motivation, who get enjoyment from the act of doing a particular thing rather than the promise of some reward later on, tend to experience flow states as a result — and are more likely to achieve their long-term goals. Not only that, but they're much happier doing it.

—   The happiest people spend much time in a state of flow, the state in which people are so involved in an activity that nothing else seems to matter.

Just look at their zygomaticus major muscles.

DON'T THINK — PEDAL

Here's Chris Powici, poet, describing his experience of cycling in flow.

 Two oystercatchers and a curlew a few feet apart on the shore, quite still, neither feeding nor calling. A dark burn running under the road from the woods onto the beach and into the sunlit tide. Raymond carver's phrase about water coming together with other water...

I'm a poet but these lines are a long way from poetry. They're no more than a wee list of some things I saw, and something I remembered, as I cycled up the west coast of the Cowal peninsula on a chilly, bright January morning. As far as I'm concerned, they're not even thoughts, maybe not even observations; an observation feels like such a deliberate sort of act. They're just some things that happened along the way — the birds, the burn and the sea, even the line from Raymond Carver's poem that popped into my head.

I like this kind of 'happening'. When I'm out on the bike the last thing I want to do is actually think. I don't cycle to consider things or find the answer to a question. Cycling is my way to stop thinking.
But that doesn't mean it's mindless. When it goes well, a certain rhythm, a kind of mind–and–body dance gets going where I feel the world more keenly. I guess you could call this a state of alertness but, importantly, this state includes memory as well. I didn't think the memory of the poem into my head. It was already there, waiting for me. The oystercatchers, curlew, the soft dazzle of sunlight, Raymond Carver's glorious description of water — the outside and inside worlds — came together because there wasn't any thinking to get in the way. I was just pedalling. Just looking.

Cycling is the finest way I know of creating this feeling of openness. Your senses are fine–tuned for the unexpected and the surprising, even if a Scottish shoreline is a perfectly natural place to come across oystercatchers and curlews. Put differently, I open myself to the shock of the familiar, the world that lies just beyond the bundle of doubts and worries that, most of time, make up most who I am. I may not be composing a poem but, by 'just looking' (and listening), I'm fulfilling a poet's first duty to the world about them. I'm noticing stuff, I'm paying attention. I'm gathering materials, the impressions of a moment, that may find their way into a poem, days, weeks or even years from now.

I'm not a quick cyclist. That January morning cycling up the wonderfully lonely Loch Stryven road, I was doing maybe nine miles an hour, roughly the same speed as a trotting roe deer or scampering fox. The kind of speed that's somewhere between walking and driving and way better than both. Confined to a car you don't get to feel the clean, cold January air in your hair or on your skin, and you don't have time to linger on the 'small stuff' — birds wading on a winter beach, the trickle of burn water. You're going too quick. The mystery of distance is lost.

Walkers will, of course, stake a big claim for the joy of striding. After all, didn't Wordsworth himself compose poems while out for a stroll? I might even argue with myself next time I find myself trudging across the local moor. But bear with me. Walking is altogether too considered, too close to the mental discipline of purposeful thinking. Let's face it, walking is just too damn step-by-step. It doesn't have that sense of release, of simple grace that comes with freewheeling or simply going with the flow of a wind-at-your-back ride along a flat, traffic-free shore road.

Cycling is all about legs and lungs, balance and sway. And it's about how, by leaning on the handlebar and turning your legs, you feel time differently. You feel an intense, more expansive sense of 'now'. The present and the past infiltrate one another. The palpable reality of birds and sunlight encounters the shifting currents of memory — when water comes together with other water, as Raymond Carver put it. I don't know how often he got a bike from the shed and found himself pedalling his local roads, but I reckon he knew all about how world and soul connect with one another, if you let them.

But there's a danger I'm getting out of my depth here. All this fancy talk of memory and connection, of soul and world, comes rather too close to thinking. I need to feel the breeze on my face and pedals under my feet. I need to let go of all this heavy duty brain-work and go for a ride.

Those who are extremely anxious wear themselves out —
become, in a sense, their own executioners.
John Calvin, theologian

Flow theory says that in order to enter a flow state, three things have to be true. According to the model described by Csikszentmihalyi:

1. THE ACTIVITY MUST HAVE CLEAR AND MEANINGFUL GOALS

That sounds rather counter–intuitive when we've spent so much time talking about not focusing on outcomes. But the goals here can be as simple as caring about the task in hand. A musician might care about playing or creating a pleasing piece of music; an artist about painting a picture; and a Mental Cyclist about experiencing an enjoyable but challenging ride.

The goal must matter to you. If it's something imposed upon you, you're unlikely to enter a flow state. That's why so many of us experience the complete opposite of flow during our day jobs. Instead of losing track of time, we're painfully aware of how slowly it's moving.

2. THERE MUST BE CLEAR AND IMMEDIATE FEEDBACK

Feedback tells you how well you're doing and enables you to adjust your performance to maintain the flow state. The musician gets feedback by listening to the music, and the artist by looking at the work they're creating. On your bike, you get feedback from your body and your senses (as well as more specific feedback from your computer stats).

3. THE CHALLENGE AND YOUR SKILLS SHOULD MATCH

If the task is too hard or if it isn't challenging enough, you won't enter a flow state. That applies not just to your actual skills but to your *perceived* skills. If you don't think you're good enough to do it, you're less likely to enter a flow state, even if your skills really are up to the job.

CREATING A POSITIVE FEEDBACK LOOP

In addition to a three-step model of flow, there's also a slightly more complex one. It's usually expressed in graph form, like this.

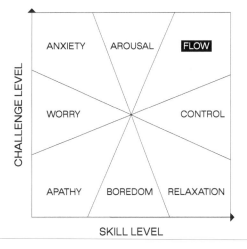

As you can see, there are two axes on the graph. The vertical axis is the challenge level of the task, which runs from low skill level (it's a doddle) to high (it's tough). The horizontal axis is your skill level, which again runs from low (you're still on stabilisers) to high (you're a skilled cyclist).

Flow is the cheerful segment that takes up the top right-hand corner of the graph. That's where the elements align to get you into the zone. It's challenging up there, but your skills are up to the task. Your skill level matches the challenge level.

Look what happens when the two axes aren't matched, though. If the skill level is low but the challenge level is medium, you're in a worried state. Ramp up the challenge level and you move into anxiety. Similarly, if the skill level is medium but the challenge level is low, you'll be apathetic or bored.

When the challenge is appropriate to your skill level — and when you are confident about those skills — you reap all kinds of rewards. Flow makes you physically calmer and emotionally happier. It keeps you completely in the moment. It frees you from distractions, makes the outside world disappear, and silences your *Cruel Critic*'s crazy chatter.

Here's Susan Cain, author of *Quiet: The Power of Introverts in a World That Can't Stop Talking*:

— Flow is an optimal state in which you feel totally engaged in an activity... in a state of flow, you're neither bored nor anxious, and you don't question your own adequacy.

As we've discovered, flow states don't happen when you're well within your comfort zone. They occur when you're pushing yourself that little bit harder. Not so hard that your experience becomes miserable, but hard enough so that there's an element of challenge to it.

This creates a positive feedback loop. The conditions that lead to a flow state are also the conditions that lead to improved performance (because you're pushing yourself a little beyond your comfort zone) and improved motivation (because the experience itself is intrinsically enjoyable, so you'll want to do it again).

Sounds good? That's mental cycling. It's about focusing on the here and now, riding wholly in the moment, and being connected to the experience. When you do that, you'll enjoy the journey, irrespective of the outcome.

I BELIEVE YOU CAN CREATE THE ZONE. THE ZONE IS A PSYCHOLOGICAL STATE. IT IS WHEN YOU ARE FOCUSED, DISCIPLINED, AND FULLY ENGAGED IN THE PROCESS AT HAND... (IT) WILL CERTAINLY INCREASE YOUR CAPACITY TO PERFORM AND SUCCEED.

ARI KIEV, PSYCHIATRIST

You can't force flow, but you can enable the conditions that make it more likely. For this exercise, I'd like you to think back to the last time you lost track of time because you were in a flow state on your bike. This will be a situation when you experienced intrinsic enjoyment in what you were doing, and were completely and utterly lost in the moment. What were the conditions that enabled you to enter that flow state?

SITUATION
What was different about this particular ride?

_____

_____

_____

_____

_____

_____

_____

CHALLENGE
How did the level of challenge correspond to your resources?

_____

_____

_____

_____

_____

_____

_____

FEELING

How did you feel during the experience, both physically and mentally?

_____

_____

_____

_____

_____

_____

_____

REPEAT

What can you do to feel this way again? How can you change your rides?

_____

_____

_____

_____

_____

_____

_____

_____

— People who are intrinsically motivated when they're doing something are more likely to enter flow states, and also more likely to achieve their long-term goals.

— You're unlikely to enter a flow state if your goal isn't meaningful to you.

— Flow occurs when the challenge and your abilities are well matched. If the challenge is too easy, you'll be bored; too hard, and you'll be agitated.

— If you focus on the here and now, you'll love the ride, regardless of where you're going.

NOTES

Looking back over this stage, what have you learned about yourself?

1.

2.

3.

THE MENTAL CYCLIST MANIFESTO
STAGE 11

ESCALATE
YOUR EXPERTISE

11.01　　DIGGING DEEP

At the beginning of the book, I discussed the importance of keeping a journal. I don't recommend journaling because I like paperwork. I recommend it because every time you reflect on how you *felt* during a ride or training session, you learn something about yourself. Every single time.

The tool for this reflection is a ride report. Here's how to do that, using (of course) a MENTAL acronym.

—	MEMORY	What happened today?
—	EVALUATE	What was important about this ride?
—	NAME	Capture and name significant emotions.
—	TRANSFORM / TREASURE	What would you like to change or repeat?
—	ACTIONS	What will you do as a result of this ride?
—	LEARNING	What did you learn about yourself?

11.02　　KATE'S RIDE JOURNAL

Let's see a worked example. Here's Kate, who had a particularly tough time in Tenerife recently. The first step, re-running your ride, is something you can do in your head. Kate has written down her thought process for us so we can understand where her head was at.

MEMORY

I'd taken my daughter Eva, who's 19, to Tenerife for a winter break, with the intention of cycling up Mount Teide together. I knew it was a tough climb, and I was anxious that I hadn't been on my bike for a few months, but I've climbed loads of mountains in my time, so I wasn't too concerned. I was a bit more concerned about Eva. She's only just taken up cycling, and this would be her first really big challenge. I thought maybe I'd been a bit too ambitious tackling Teide — it's Europe's longest continuous ascent, after all! — but I was planning to support her carefully if she found it tough.

She's a competitive lass, so I knew there was no point suggesting we didn't have to go to the very top. Plus, halfway measures are not really my thing either.

Anyway, I couldn't have been more wrong to be worried. Eva flew up the mountain! I can't have ridden with her for more than twenty minutes as we climbed from the coast. When we hit the road to the top, she left me for dead.

Dead was how I felt. Teide was one of those rides where you discover things about yourself. Things you don't want to know, like these days I apparently have to push when the gradient goes over 8%. I wore out my bloody cleats pushing my bloody bike up that bloody hill! I've never pushed before.

I felt really frustrated and angry with myself for getting so out of shape. I was knackered from the beginning. The more knackered I got, the more stressed I became. I wasn't sure I'd be able to get to the top at all, even pushing.

It was no fun at all. I tried chunking it up and riding bend to bend, rewarding any progress with sips of water and Jelly Babies, but there were so many times I just had to stop and get off and push.

I lost count of how many people rode past me. A few asked how I was doing, and I just felt embarrassed. I'm the girl who rides past other people! And of course I was wearing my Tourmalet jersey, a souvenir from past triumphs, so I felt ridiculous. A fraud. All the gear, no idea. Plus this jersey used to be a great fit and now my belly was bulging through it. Ugh.

Worse, I hadn't made any plans with Eva about where to meet because I hadn't expected her to ride ahead of me. Would she know to wait for me at the summit? Was there even an obvious summit with a sign so she'd know?

And then I ran out of water. Teide is a volcano, and I couldn't see any springs. I was miles from the nearest village.

Now I was beginning to panic. What if Eva was also out of water? I'd tried many times to call and message her but there was no signal up here. What if I couldn't find her? What if she'd had an accident and was lying in pain waiting for me? What if there was a fork in the road and she'd gone one way and I went the other? My imagination went into overdrive. I knew I had to keep going, but my anxiety just made it harder. Which made me feel worse.

Icouldn'tdothis.Myclimbingdayswereobviouslyover,andIwasaterriblemother. I dumped my bike on the verge and sat on a wall in the sunshine. If it wasn't for Eva, I'd have rolled straight back down to our all-inclusive hotel and pigged out on pastries. It was all I felt good for. But that wasn't an option. I knew I had to keep going one way or another.

EVALUATE | NAME | TRANSFORM / TREASURE

You can do these three steps in one hit. First, Kate wrote down three negative and three positive things that happened. It's curious that none of the positives appeared in her memory of the ride. She only remembered the good stuff when she had to focus on the positives as part of the exercise.

Then she put a name to her feelings. Finally, she identified how she'd rather feel in the negative experiences (transform) and what she'd like to take away from the positive ones (treasure).

EVALUATE	NEGATIVE	NAME	TRANSFORM
I had to push. A lot.	Angry (with myself).	Confident about my fitness.
I lost contact with Eva and didn't have a plan.	Panicky.	Confident I had a plan for every eventuality.
I didn't think I could do it.	Miserable!	Confident I could do it.

EVALUATE	POSITIVE	NAME	TREASURE
I met a cool girl from Belgium who was also struggling. She told me she'd been using me as a marker and finally caught up when I'd stopped for the 100th time. We had a good laugh and rode on together. That helped.	Friendship.	Remember cycling is social and lots of lovely people do it.
When I finally got to the top, Eva was waiting for me. We had a big hug and took in the views. They were absolutely stunning.	Happy.	Special moments with Eva.
The descent was awesome!	Exhilarated!	Train properly so I can enjoy the uphills as well as the downhills.

ACTIONS

Kate might have focused on developing a training regime, bought a turbo trainer, and grown legs of steel. But her considered response was much simpler.

> *I want to spend much more time cycling with Eva, so I'm going to plan to make that happen!*

LEARNING

So often, we shrug off bad experiences and fail to make the most of good experiences. In this final step, the goal is to reflect on what you've learned and continuously increase your expertise in yourself. Here's Kate:

> *I need to be realistic about my fitness, and not take on more than I can do. The rewards of the view at the top and the amazing descent didn't compensate sufficiently for the hell of the ascent! I also need to prepare properly for rides, especially with Eva. I've never been so scared on a bike. Above all, I'm happy to acknowledge that I'm much more motivated by the social side of cycling than by crazy performance targets.*

Mastering others is strength.
Mastering yourself is true power.
Lao Tzu, philosopher

Mental cycling is about getting to know yourself better. There's no better way to do this than by reflecting on a ride. I can't recommend ride reports highly enough. Complete this exercise after your next ride, and then repeat frequently. The more you do, the more you'll learn — and the bigger the benefits.

MEMORY
What happened today?

EVALUATE | NAME x TRANSFORM OR TREASURE
What happened today?

EVALUATE | NEGATIVE	NAME	TRANSFORM
1.		
2.		
3.		

EVALUATE | POSITIVE	NAME	TREASURE
1.		
2.		
3.		

ACTION
What will I do now?

LEARNING
What have I learned about myself?

— Mental cycling is about getting to know yourself better.

— There's no better way to do that than by reflecting on your rides as they happen.

— The more you learn about yourself, the more you can use that to change the way you think — and change the way you ride.

NOTES

Looking back over this stage, what have you learned about yourself?

1. ....

....

....

....

....

....

2. ....

....

....

....

....

....

3. ....

....

....

....

....

....

THE MENTAL CYCLIST MANIFESTO
STAGE 12

COMMIT TO
YOUR CHALLENGE

I suggested right at the start that goals are important. They motivate us to do stuff and, if we're smart about it, can help us focus on doing the *right* stuff.

You'll find goal setting in many people's success stories. Sometimes, there's a correlation between the ambition of the goal and the scope of the success. It really can pay to think big.

For example, when he was a (spud-faced) nipper, the footballer Wayne Rooney took goal setting literally. He imagined scoring what he called "wonder goals". These are the kind of goals that get an entire stadium applauding in awe. The kind of goals that get you through early morning training sessions and games in the pouring rain.

VISUALISING SUCCESS

It's not just sportspeople. In his pre-fame days, comedian Jim Carrey wrote himself a blank cheque for 10 million dollars, payable to himself for "acting services rendered". He dated it ten years in the future and used that cheque to remind himself of what he wanted to be — an incredibly successful comedian — when he was struggling to get any bookings at all.

And Sara Blakey, founder of the Spanx shapewear empire, didn't imagine spreadsheets full of big numbers when she was struggling to start her business. She imagined appearing on Oprah as a self-made success. Which, of course, she went on to do.

It's time to focus on your next cycling goal. Let's call it your Mental Cyclist Challenge. Your challenge might be nailing KOMs in the Pyrenees, or riding 100 miles for the first time, or commuting to the office, or racing around the world. It might just be getting out and about in the fresh air more regularly because a bike is a lot more fun than the gym.

Everyone's challenge will, and should be, different and personal. But the process for finding the right challenge for you can be the same for everyone, regardless of age, ability, ambition, or anything else. It starts with thinking about some things you'd love to do.

DON'T LIMIT YOUR CHALLENGES. CHALLENGE YOUR LIMITS.

TONY ROBBINS, AUTHOR

List three Do Goals now. That's three things you want to do, or three potential challenges you might want to set yourself, or three milestones you want to achieve. It doesn't matter what they are or how you express them. What matters is that each one involves doing something that has a clearly defined outcome.

For example:

— Complete a particular ride.
— Set a new personal best.
— Lose a specified amount of weight.
— Reach the top of a leader board.
— Ride 100 miles in a day.
— Tour a country.
— Take a year out to ride around the world.

I WANT TO ....

THIS WILL BE MEANINGFUL TO ME BECAUSE:

THIS WILL BE REWARDING FOR ME BECAUSE:

I WANT TO ....

THIS WILL BE MEANINGFUL TO ME BECAUSE:

THIS WILL BE REWARDING FOR ME BECAUSE:

I WANT TO ....

THIS WILL BE MEANINGFUL TO ME BECAUSE:

THIS WILL BE REWARDING FOR ME BECAUSE:

To definitely decide on your Mental Cyclist Challenge, you're now going to think about things a little bit differently.

In *The Hitch-Hiker's Guide To The Galaxy*, a hyper-intelligent, highly evolved alien species builds a supercomputer to calculate the Ultimate Answer to the Ultimate Question of Life, The Universe and Everything. It's a massive project that requires incredible amounts of money and manpower. And once the supercomputer has been built, it will take a bit of time to work out the answer.

Millions and millions of years. Eventually, the computer, named Deep Thought, finishes its calculations. The answer to life, the universe and everything is...

42.

The aliens' ancestors are horrified. They waited millions of years for... this? But Deep Thought has checked, and checked, and checked again. The answer is most definitely 42.

The problem, it turns out, isn't the answer. The answer is fine. The problem is the question.

START WITH WHY

The people who built Deep Thought to answer the Ultimate Question didn't know what the Ultimate Question was. And because they didn't understand the question, the answer is completely meaningless.

But there's a solution. They can build a computer even more powerful than Deep Thought and ask it to work out what the Ultimate Question actually is. It'll only take a few million more years.

It's a funny story, but it's a serious point: just as there's no point in answering a question that you don't really understand, there's no point in setting out to do something if you don't know why you want to do it. That's just a recipe for stress, for strain, and for potential disaster.

Understanding why you want to do something will save you an awful lot of effort chasing things that aren't what you really want.

12.03   ADD THE WHY

You've made a list of some things you want to do. These are your Do Goals. Now it's time to work out what question you're actually answering. *Why* do you want to do these things? Why do you want to climb that hill, enter that race, ride a million miles, achieve that objective, tackle that challenge?

Earlier, we discussed the importance of having goals that really matter to you — goals that you find meaningful and rewarding. We also considered performance and enjoyment as key factors in goal setting. So, let's bear that in mind and do a bit of mental time travel.

FUTURE GAZING

Take your Three Mental Breaths and look at the three Do Goals you've just written down. Now travel forwards in your mind to the moment when you've just completed each one. Put yourself at the summit or on the podium or in the pub after the ride. You've done it!

Now, be really honest with yourself. This is a thought experiment rather than a written exercise.

—   How do you feel in this moment?
—   Why was the goal meaningful?
—   How was it rewarding?

If you're not 100% convinced that this is as good as it gets on a bicycle, consider it a lucky escape. If you're not blown away by your achievement in a thought experiment, how would you feel when you're also dealing with physical tiredness and all the other challenges that go with it?

There's no point in wasting your time and your energy on something that doesn't really matter to you.

Challenges are what make life interesting.
Overcoming them is what makes life meaningful.
Joshua J Marine, author (allegedly)

BE RUTHLESS

Do Goals are not like children: it's okay to swap them. Sometimes the goals we had a few years, months, or even weeks ago are no longer so important to us. Sometimes even the biggest, most longstanding ambitions turn out to be a lot less attractive when we think critically about them.

Our Do Goals are set in the future. They're just stories we tell ourselves. That means we're free to follow the same advice that other kinds of storytellers follow:

— Kill your darlings.

That's a quote from American author William Faulkner, and it means that sometimes the best way to make a story better is to get rid of the bit you want to keep the most. It could be a particular character, a really great bit of description, a sub-plot... whatever it is, by hanging on to it you're stopping yourself from telling the best possible story.

If any one of your Do Goals isn't meaningful and rewarding, kill it. Don't hesitate. Don't settle for less than you should. If they all leave you lukewarm, blow them all up.

12.04   DO-BE-DO-BE-DO

When we talk about goals, particularly cycling goals, we tend to talk about things we're going to do:

— I'm going to climb that mountain.
— I'm going to ride that sportive.
— I'm going to enter that race.
— I'm going to circumnavigate this planet.

That's what you've just done, of course. A Do Goal is something specific with a clearly defined outcome. Do Goals are fine and can be super motivating. But there is a danger here. They're all about the 'what', and not about the 'why'.

FOOLS RUSH IN

Have you ever set your mind to do something that seemed like a killer idea at the time but which, on reflection, turned out to be not so great after all? You know the kind of thing — someone suggests a challenge and you agree instinctively, without really considering why you'd want to do it. Then one day, when you're halfway through training and feeling strangely empty about the whole thing, a little voice starts to make itself heard:

- — Why exactly are you doing this?
- — Why do you care about this?
- — Are you sure you really want to do this?
- — Are you really sure?
- — Really?
- — REALLY?

Now you're not just dealing with the physical demands of preparing for your adventure. You're also battling mental pressures that force you to question whether you want to have this adventure at all. That voice — yes, your *Yeah, But* voice — will find a hundred different ways to question your commitment and convince you that you're not really up to the job. It'll tell you that you don't really care about the outcome. It wants you to believe that all your training is a waste of time, so you might as well go and do something else instead. Something you'd enjoy.

It's a bit like doing a track–stand on ice. If you really concentrate, if you really put lots of effort in, you might be able to wobble around and keep your balance — for a while. But sooner or later, you're going to end up on your arse.

THE FEELS OF WHEELS

Here's Kevin MacNeil, lecturer, poet, playwright and screenwriter, describing the powerful emotional benefits of cycling. You may recognise yourself in his description.

> *If I had to give everyone on the planet an inessential material gift, I would give them a set of wheels. Do not underestimate wheels. Anything that cannot be reinvented is fundamental. Civilised life thrives on wheels. Prams. Cars. Wheelchairs. Bikes.*
>
> *When I started cycling, some years ago, I was living in a simple draughty cottage on a weatherful island in the extreme north. In my mid–thirties, I'd had a broken–hearted, broken–minded kind of life I often thought of writing about, though the sheer scale of the ask — not to mention its potential egotism — defeated me. In fact, in Shetland as a writer in residence, I hadn't, for a long time, been able to write anything. Pressed down by the weight of my own flaws, I had felt blank and hopeless. Until the bike.*
>
> *I bought it on a whim. It was new, a sleek black machine that fascinated me. An artist once said that the bike is a "surrealist invention", that cycling is "a surreal way of walking". The bike was a work of art. It symbolised freedom. Here was art with a commensurate practical value, like a novel that cheers you up, taking you up and away out of yourself.*

I went swooping through Shetland's wind-scoured contours, with its ever-changing sea views and enormous wheeling sky, and the elements united in rhythm: my heart and the bike and my legs and the road and my lungs and the wind. The very cadence of things actual and things perceived melded. Cycling was like a drug. But a nourishing, healing one.

I pared my crestfallen life down to essences — eating, drinking, sleeping, reading, writing, cycling, meditating. My ennui slowly lifted. I began to feel more confident, more connected, more joyful. And my creativity returned. I found myself not only fulfilling my current writing projects, but attracting new commissions too.

I later lived in London and cycled three or four times around Richmond Park most days to maintain my equilibrium. And to help me write. Wheels love the imagination. Bike-riding hypnotises you, even while demanding a Zen-like mindfulness. The landscape blurs past and the movement seems to give a more adventurous shape to thought patterns. Cycling — often, though far from exclusively, a solitary pursuit — has helped me to feel engaged with the world, a sense that can often elude writers, typing away in their insular bubbles. On my bike, I feel part of something bigger.

I've harnessed that awareness into trying to help others by cycling for charity. I rode 1,300km of the Danube, from its very source to Budapest, to raise money for cancer charities, and later I cycled from the north of the Isle of Lewis to the south of the Isle of Harris, in my native Outer Hebrides, for the hospice where my mother spent her final weeks. Always on a fixed-gear bike.

Now I cycle as often as I can. I ride my bike to work, no matter what the weather is like. Learning to look after and fix mechanical issues gave me confidence. I'm working with colleagues at the university where I teach to investigate not only how physical activity such as cycling affect wellbeing, but also how writing might help athletes cope with the stresses related to performance and the difficulties faced when a sporting career has run its course and the spotlight has turned its enthusiastic eye on to someone else.

It is years since I owned a car. The rise in cycling's popularity makes me happy. I quietly gladden when I see others cycling: giddy toddlers on trikes, eager teens on mountain bikes, cosmopolitan renegades on fashionable fixies, senior citizens on tandems sharing rich memories and late-life heartbeats. They all understand cycling's open secret — that it encourages us to get more out of life, to be healthier in body and mind.

Cycling should be about how you feel, not what you do. Mental cycling is ALL about how you feel. We need some Feel Goals. Let's meet someone you haven't seen, or been, for a very long time. I'd like you to think back to when you were five.

When you were five, you could do anything. Your ideas were as big as the sky. You might decide one day that you're going to be an explorer or a doctor, an astronaut, or a vet. Maybe you'll be the world's only space vet explorer, flying around the universe treating sick animals nobody has ever seen before.

When you're five, you're full of heroic, magical ideas. What happened next? Life happened next. Life told you:

—   NOPE.

Life told you that there aren't any animals in space. That you're too short to be an astronaut. That your country doesn't have a space programme anyway. The longer you lived, the less magical your thinking became. And that's a shame — but that five-year-old is still inside you.

WE CAN BE HEROES

I'm not going to ask you to role-play being five or anything creepy like that. But I am going to ask you to imagine what you'd feel like today if life hadn't told you 'no' so many times.

—   What kind of cyclist would you be?

—   What kind of cycling challenge would thrill you — really *thrill* you — if you'd never developed any limiting beliefs about what you could do?

—   What would your goals be now if you still had that magical thinking and that heroic mindset?

This is probably not the kind of thinking you normally do. But what a pity that is, because the consequences of indulging your inner five-year-old can be amazing. So let's go do that now.

Your imagination is your preview to life's
coming attractions.
Albert Einstein, genius

This is a visualisation exercise designed to help you feel the way you should feel on a perfect bike ride. If you would like to do this as a guided exercise, which many people find really helpful, listen to the audio session on the website here: mentalcyclist.com/resources.

If you'd prefer just to follow this abbreviated text, get yourself somewhere comfy and quiet for the next few minutes. Read through the steps below and do them in your own time.

STEP 1

Take your Three Mental Breaths and relax.

Release your imagination and picture the most incredible, most exciting, most enjoyable bike ride you could possibly experience. Visualise every detail. Every sight and every sound. Every smell and every sensation. Can you feel your hands on the bars? Your feet in the pedals? Your bum on the saddle? Can you feel the air on your face? Can you hear the tyres on the road? What can you see up ahead?

Imagine you can do anything, be anywhere. Forget practical. Forget affordable. Forget realistic. There's no "I can't". No "I shouldn't". No "I won't". You're a perfect person in a perfect world.

Soak up the sensations from your senses and feel yourself on your bike. You're in a deep state of flow. Experience your ride with the mind of a five-year old who knows that anything is possible. No barriers, no filters. You're a Mental Cyclist. Let your imagination ride free.

STEP 2

When you're ready, ease yourself out of your visualisation. Remember your feelings, and sit with them for a moment or two. Now gently ask yourself:

—   How do I feel about myself right now?

That's the way you should always feel, right? So let's call it your Feel Goal. Capture your amazing feeling right now so you can always refer to it. I'm not going to give you any prompts about what you might say because this should come straight from your gut in your own words.

I am the greatest. I said that even before
I knew I was.
Muhammad Ali, boxer

I FEEL

We've looked at Do Goals and Feel Goals independently. Now we need to match them up and find your Mental Cyclist Challenge. Two quick thoughts first.

DON'T BE DULL

When you were thinking about your five-year-old self having a wonderful ride, did your feelings express themselves as Key Performance Indicators? Or perhaps as Specific Measurable Achievable Realistic Targets? No? How about Actionable Insights?

Of course not, because there's nothing like a bit of management jargon to suck the life out of anything. Five-year-old you would, quite rightly, have found this stuff boring. The grown-up you should find them boring too. Boring goals are your enemy. Nobody ever leapt out of bed full of excitement at the prospect of trying to make their day 12.17% better. Your Mental Cyclist Challenge should make you feel absolutely amazing!

DO BE HONEST

When you were thinking about why your Do Goals matter to you, did you write something like this?

—   It would be a really special achievement that I've dreamed of for years, and I'd be so proud of myself for doing it!

Or was your thought process more like this?

—   That fit, smug guy at the gym did it last year, and he's older than me, so I want to prove I can do it too.

If so, it won't wash. Not when push comes to shove and the training begins to hurt. You'll convince yourself fairly easily that you don't really care about the fit, smug guy at the gym. And nor, of course, should you.

Here's the simple truth. When your Do Goals are meaningful and rewarding to you precisely because of how they make you feel, and that feeling is deeply important to you, you'll be incredibly motivated to take on any challenge.

When you think like a child your imagination
is free and anything is possible.
Criss Angel, magician

RIGHT IN THE FEELS

So are you ready to commit to your Mental Cyclist Challenge? All you have to do is take your Feel Goal and find the ultimate Do Goal to help you achieve it. This might be one of your Do Goals from the earlier exercise, but it doesn't have to be. If your current Do Goals are not a perfect fit for how you want to feel, find better ones. Then find the best one.

What's the most exciting challenge you could set yourself that would make you feel truly amazing? Something that's fully aligned with everything you've learned and worked through in The Mental Cyclist?

MY MENTAL CYCLIST CHALLENGE

PART 3
YOUR MENTAL CYCLIST CHALLENGE

EYE ON THE PRIZE

The benefit of splitting big goals into smaller goals is that small goals are less daunting. If you want to lose 10 kilos in body mass, it's more helpful to set yourself weekly targets that feel achievable (challenges) than to constantly focus on a scary target that feels way beyond you (definitely a threat). One day at a time (sweet Jesus), and all that. Sweat the small stuff, and in no time at all you'll burn through the blubber and hit your big goal.

That's the theory. Bin it. You don't need it. It's a sleight of hand designed to take your mind off the big picture. You're a Mental Cyclist now. You don't need to fool anybody — least of all yourself. You've never been more motivated to achieve something extraordinary and exciting in your life!

Which is not to say you shouldn't chunk up your challenge. You absolutely should, because it's a really smart way of maintaining your focus and tracking your progress. The difference is that you're not trying to avoid thinking about the big goal. Contemplate and celebrate your Mental Cyclist Challenge every single day!

In this section, you're going to complete a 12–week tracker. Here's what to do.

1. CREATE A ROUTE MAP

Decide when you're going to do your Mental Cyclist Challenge. You may already know, but if not give yourself a deadline. Be as precise as possible. 'Someday, maybe' won't cut it.

Since your challenge is some way beyond your current comfort zone (or certainly should be — Mental Cyclists don't do beige), you're going to have to work towards it. You might need to get fitter or build up your endurance riding, for example. So, chunk up the time between today and your challenge, and set yourself three milestone dates. We're working on a 12–week plan, so the dates should be:

Milestone 1:	4 weeks from now.
Milestone 2:	8 weeks from now.
Milestone 3:	12 weeks from now (just before you ~~tackle~~ smash your challenge).

Then, for each milestone date, assign three key goals. These will be things like:

— Increase your training to three days a week.
— Hit a weekly ride target of 100 miles.
— Undertake a training program with a PT.
— Improve your endurance by doing three rides over 50 miles.
— Do yoga daily for flexibility and recovery.
— Increase your FTP by 15%.
— Lose 5% of body weight.
— Reduce your weekly alcohol units to single digits.
— Improve your diet by eating more protein and fewer carbs.
— Learn how to fix your bike by watching videos.
— Buy a new bike.

Be specific. And be positive. Every goal should be expressed as an achievement goal, so it's "I will rock that old jersey I haven't worn for years" rather than "I will cut the carbs and lose my moobs". You might want to set yourself completely different goals for each milestone, or continue the same themes with new targets. For example, if you decide to reduce your chocolate intake to zero by the first milestone, you won't need to mention it again (unless you fall off the wagon). But if you're looking to ramp up the frequency and duration of your rides, you might set yourself ride targets for all three milestones.

Of course, you'll have lots of intermediate goals, but the trick with your big milestone goals is figuring out what's *really* important for you. You've learned a great deal about yourself on your journey with The Mental Cyclist, so you know what matters and what doesn't.

While you'll be working with a 12-week tracker, you can of course be flexible. If your challenge is more than 12 weeks away, or sooner, just flex the dates. The important thing is to keep the structure of having three milestones and three goals for each.

Do the difficult things while they are easy and do
the great things while they are small. A journey of
a thousand miles must begin with a single step.
Lao Tzu, philosopher

2. TRACK YOUR PROGRESS

By all means use apps to monitor and record your training progress. This can be highly motivating. But you won't be tracking stats here in The Mental Cyclist. That's not mental cycling territory. Instead, you'll track your feelings as you work through your milestone goals. By journaling your progress weekly in the On The Road tracker, you'll stay focussed on everything you've learned about yourself while working through The Mental Cyclist — and, of course, continue to learn. Never forget: it's your mind, not your legs, that pushes the pedals, so preparing mentally for your challenge is every bit as important as the physical stuff. More so, in fact.

3. SHARE YOUR SUCCESS

Science shows that when you share a personal commitment to do something, you're more likely to actually do it. That could be one reason for sharing your Mental Cyclist Challenge with family, friends, your social networks, and the world. But there's another, more powerful reason. When you see a cyclist with a puncture or a mechanical problem, or simply suffering from fatigue at the side of the road, you don't ride on by. You do whatever you can to help them out, whether it's offering them a tube or a gel or a wheel to follow.

Why do you check? Because you're a cyclist — and cyclists care. As a breed, we are naturally altruistic. We look after our brothers and sisters on the road (and off-road too, of course, if you're that way inclined). We want to share our brilliant sport and encourage others to join in. We want to make it as much fun as possible for everyone.

The whole point of becoming a Mental Cyclist is to do more on your bike, free from the psychological barriers that hold you back. Your Mental Cyclist Challenge is your considered expression of everything you want to do, be, and feel. I encourage you to share your commitment — not just so you feel more motivated to do it, but so you can inspire others to do the same. Visit mentalcyclist.com to join Club TMC.

Right, enough from me. On the following pages you'll find your Route Map for your challenge and your 12-week On The Road tracker. I hope you've enjoyed The Mental Cyclist, and I know you'll love your Mental Cyclist Challenge. Most of all, I look forward to hearing about your success and seeing you inspire others to change their minds to change their rides.

IF YOU WERE TO ASK
ME IF I'D EVER HAD THE
BAD LUCK TO MISS MY
DAILY COCKTAIL, I'D HAVE
TO SAY THAT I DOUBT IT;
WHERE CERTAIN THINGS
ARE CONCERNED,
I PLAN AHEAD.

LUIS BUÑUEL, FILM-MAKER

MY MENTAL CYCLIST CHALLENGE | ROUTE MAP

MILESTONE 1 DATE ....

GOAL 1

Why this is important

GOAL 2

Why this is important

GOAL 3

Why this is important

MILESTONE 2   DATE _____   **MILESTONE 3**   DATE _____

YOU HAVE TO TRAIN YOUR MIND AS MUCH AS YOUR BODY.

VENUS WILLIAMS,
TENNIS PLAYER

What am I going to do this week to help me achieve my goals?

	I WILL DO	TIME	I WILL FEEL
MONDAY			
TUESDAY			
WEDNESDAY			
THURSDAY			
FRIDAY			
SATURDAY			
SUNDAY			

MILESTONE 1 | **ON THE ROAD** DATE ....

I feel good about myself because:

1 ....

2 ....

3 ....

Are you comparing yourself to others? ☐ YES ☐ NO

How can you let go of this thinking? ....

....

....

Are you winning all your willpower wars? ☐ YES ☐ NO

What one thing can you do to defeat your *Yeah, But* voice? ....

....

....

How extrinsically motivated are you to achieve your 3 goals?

GOAL 1   MEH | ⁞ ⁞ ⁞ ⁞ ⁞ ⁞ | ⁞ ⁞ ⁞ ⁞ ⁞ | MASSIVELY!

GOAL 2   MEH | ⁞ ⁞ ⁞ ⁞ ⁞ ⁞ | ⁞ ⁞ ⁞ ⁞ ⁞ | MASSIVELY!

GOAL 3   MEH | ⁞ ⁞ ⁞ ⁞ ⁞ ⁞ | ⁞ ⁞ ⁞ ⁞ ⁞ | MASSIVELY!

What one change can you make to maximise your motivation? ....

....

....

Thinking about your 3 goals for this milestone, how confident are you of success?

GOAL 1   YIKES! | | | | | | | | | | | | | | | | YAY!

GOAL 2   YIKES! | | | | | | | | | | | | | | | | YAY!

GOAL 3   YIKES! | | | | | | | | | | | | | | | | YAY!

How can you adapt your goals or training to have more fun? _____

_____

_____

Create 3 mantras using the words below, or your own. Use the I AM or YOU ARE format...

☐ STRONG   ☐ CAPABLE   ☐ FAST   ☐ LOVING IT!

☐ ENOUGH   ☐ CALM   ☐ CONFIDENT   ☐ FEARLESS

☐ A WINNER   ☐ DETERMINED   ☐ _____   ☐ _____

How will your mantras help you on your next ride? _____

_____

_____

Do you feel stressed
about your goals?   I GOT THE FEAR | | | | | | | | | | | | | | | | I GOT THIS

What one thing can you do to shake off the stress? _____

_____

Mental Cyclists feel the fun. List 3 things you love about your cycling:

I LOVE _____

I LOVE _____

I LOVE _____

YOUR BODY DRIVES YOU TO THE LINE. BUT YOUR MIND MAKES YOU CROSS IT.

SEBASTIAN KIENLE, TRIATHLETE

What am I going to do this week to help me achieve my goals?

	I WILL DO	TIME	I WILL FEEL
MONDAY			
TUESDAY			
WEDNESDAY			
THURSDAY			
FRIDAY			
SATURDAY			
SUNDAY			

MILESTONE 1 **ON THE ROAD**   DATE ....

I feel good about myself because:

1 ....

2 ....

3 ....

Are you aware of any true and important limiting beliefs?   ☐ YES   ☐ NO

How can you challenge these or work around the ones you can't change? ....

....

....

Do you perceive your milestone goals as challenges or threats?

GOAL 1   PUPPY | ¦ ¦ ¦ ¦ ¦ ¦ | ¦ ¦ ¦ ¦ ¦ | BEAR

GOAL 2   PUPPY | ¦ ¦ ¦ ¦ ¦ ¦ | ¦ ¦ ¦ ¦ ¦ | BEAR

GOAL 3   PUPPY | ¦ ¦ ¦ ¦ ¦ ¦ | ¦ ¦ ¦ ¦ ¦ | BEAR

How can you move from threat to challenge? ....

....

....

How attached are you to targets?   WHATEVER | ¦ ¦ ¦ ¦ ¦ | ¦ ¦ ¦ ¦ ¦ | WHATEVER IT TAKES!

How can you let go of attachment and find your flow? ....

....

....

For each goal, list one thing that could go wrong then consider how you will stay on track...

GOAL 1 IF ....

THEN ....

....

GOAL 2 IF ....

THEN ....

....

GOAL 3 IF ....

THEN ....

....

What are you loving right now as you work towards your goals ? ....

....

....

What one change can you make to feel more fun? ....

....

....

Mental Cyclists have a heroic mindset. Therefore:

I AM ....

I CAN ....

I WILL ....

WHEN YOU BECOME THE IMAGE OF YOUR OWN IMAGINATION, IT'S THE MOST POWERFUL THING YOU COULD EVER DO.

RUPAUL CHARLES,
DRAG QUEEN

What am I going to do this week to help me achieve my goals?

	I WILL DO	TIME	I WILL FEEL
MONDAY			
TUESDAY			
WEDNESDAY			
THURSDAY			
FRIDAY			
SATURDAY			
SUNDAY			

DATE ....

I feel good about myself because:

1 ....

2 ....

3 ....

Have you blown up a highway with a bazooka? ☐ YES ☐ NO

What's stressing you out right now? ....

....

....

What strategies do you have for shaking off the stress? ....

....

....

Mental Cyclists are mindful. Take Three Mental Breaths, then jot down the first 3 things you notice. These could be things you see, or hear, or smell, or feel.

1 ....

2 ....

3 ....

What one change could you make to develop a more positive mindset? ....

....

....

You're close to your first milestone — great work! How confident are you of success?

GOAL 1 YIKES! | | | | | | | | | | | | | | YAY!

GOAL 2 YIKES! | | | | | | | | | | | | | | YAY!

GOAL 3 YIKES! | | | | | | | | | | | | | | YAY!

Are you winning all your willpower wars? ☐ YES ☐ NO

What is your *Yeah, But* voice telling you and how can you defeat it? _____

_____

_____

How intrinsically motivated are you to achieve your 3 goals?

GOAL 1 SHRUG | | | | | | | | | | | | | | BRING IT ON!

GOAL 2 SHRUG | | | | | | | | | | | | | | BRING IT ON!

GOAL 3 SHRUG | | | | | | | | | | | | | | BRING IT ON!

Mental Cyclists feel the fun. List 3 things you love about cycling:

1._____

2._____

3._____

PERFECTIONISM IS JUST AN EXCUSE FOR SELF CRITICISM.

SHARON MARTIN, THERAPIST

What am I going to do this week to help me achieve my goals?

	I WILL DO	TIME	I WILL FEEL
MONDAY			
TUESDAY			
WEDNESDAY			
THURSDAY			
FRIDAY			
SATURDAY			
SUNDAY			

DATE

I feel good about myself because:

1

2

3

How committed are you to your Mental Cyclist Challenge?   I'LL TRY | | | | | | | | | | | | | | | | TRY STOPPING ME!

Be honest about any wobbles you're having.

What can you do today to develop a more heroic mindset?

How loud is your Cruel Critic right now?   SILENT | | | | | | | | | | | | | | | | SCREAMING

How can you squash the self–criticism?

Are you comparing yourself to others?   ☐ YES ☐ NO

How can you let go of this thinking?

Thinking about your Mental Cyclist Challenge, how do you feel?

☐ EXCITED   ☐ DETERMINED   ☐ NERVOUS   ☐ STRONG

☐ STRESSED   ☐ CALM   ☐ CONFIDENT   ☐ INSPIRED

☐ SCARED   ☐ POSITIVE   ☐ FRUSTRATED   ☐ HAPPY

☐ LETHARGIC   ☐ ENERGETIC   ☐ UNCERTAIN   ☐ WORRIED

☐   ☐   ☐   ☐

How is your growing self-expertise helping you hit your goals?

Do you want to revise any of the milestone
goals in your Route Planner?   ☐ YES   ☐ NO

If so, how and why?

Mental Cyclists have a heroic mindset. What positive affirmations will keep you on track?

I AM

I CAN

I WILL

Congratulations! You've reached your first milestone. Before moving on, take a moment to reflect on your feelings and recognise your achievements. You did it!

Now it's time to prepare mentally for Milestone 2. Update your milestone goals here if you've made any changes so you have a clear focus for the weeks ahead.

GOAL 1

Why this is important

GOAL 2

Why this is important

GOAL 3

Why this is important

What am I going to do this week to help me achieve my goals?

	I WILL DO	TIME	I WILL FEEL
MONDAY			
TUESDAY			
WEDNESDAY			
THURSDAY			
FRIDAY			
SATURDAY			
SUNDAY			

How do you feel right now?

☐ EXCITED	☐ DETERMINED	☐ NERVOUS	☐ STRONG
☐ STRESSED	☐ CALM	☐ CONFIDENT	☐ INSPIRED
☐ SCARED	☐ POSITIVE	☐ SORE	☐ HAPPY
☐	☐	☐	☐

Are you comparing yourself to others?   ☐ YES ☐ NO

How can you let go of this thinking? ....

....

....

Are you winning all your willpower wars?   ☐ YES ☐ NO

What one thing can you do to defeat your *Yeah, But* voice? ....

....

....

How extrinsically motivated are you by your 3 milestone goals?

GOAL 1	MEH		MASSIVELY!
GOAL 2	MEH		MASSIVELY!
GOAL 3	MEH		MASSIVELY!

What one change can you make to maximise your motivation? ....

....

....

Thinking about your 3 goals for this milestone, how confident are you of success?

GOAL 1   YIKES! | | | | | | | | | | YAY!

GOAL 2   YIKES! | | | | | | | | | | YAY!

GOAL 3   YIKES! | | | | | | | | | | YAY!

How can you adapt your goals or training to have more fun? _____

_____

_____

How do you feel right now?

☐ STRONG   ☐ CAPABLE   ☐ FAST   ☐ LOVING IT!

☐ ENOUGH   ☐ CALM   ☐ CONFIDENT   ☐ FEARLESS

☐ A WINNER   ☐ DETERMINED   ☐ _____   ☐ _____

How will your mantras help you on your next ride? _____

_____

_____

Do you feel stressed
about your goals?   I GOT THE FEAR | | | | | | | | | | I GOT THIS

What one thing can you do to shake off the stress? _____

_____

Mental Cyclists feel the fun. List 3 things you love about your cycling:

I LOVE _____

I LOVE _____

I LOVE _____

MINDFULNESS ISN'T DIFFICULT. WE JUST NEED TO REMEMBER TO DO IT.

SHARON SALZBERG,
AUTHOR

What am I going to do this week to help me achieve my goals?

	I WILL DO	TIME	I WILL FEEL
MONDAY			
TUESDAY			
WEDNESDAY			
THURSDAY			
FRIDAY			
SATURDAY			
SUNDAY			

DATE ....

I feel good about myself because:

1 ....

2 ....

3 ....

Are you aware of any true and important limiting beliefs? ☐ YES ☐ NO

How can you challenge these or work around the ones you can't change? ....

....

....

Do you perceive your milestone goals as challenges or threats?

GOAL 1	PUPPY												BEAR
GOAL 2	PUPPY												BEAR
GOAL 3	PUPPY												BEAR

How can you move from threat to challenge? ....

....

....

How attached are you to targets? WHATEVER | | | | | | | | | | | | | | WHATEVER IT TAKES!

How can you let go of attachment and find your flow? ....

....

....

For each goal, list one thing that could go wrong then consider how you will stay on track...

GOAL 1 IF _____

THEN _____

_____

GOAL 2 IF _____

THEN _____

_____

GOAL 3 IF _____

THEN _____

_____

What are you loving right now as you work towards your goals ? _____

_____

_____

What one change can you make to feel more fun? _____

_____

_____

Mental Cyclists have a heroic mindset. Therefore:

I AM _____

I CAN _____

I WILL _____

WE MUST HAVE PIE. STRESS CANNOT EXIST IN THE PRESENCE OF PIE.

DAVID MAMET, PLAYWRIGHT

What am I going to do this week to help me achieve my goals?

	I WILL DO	TIME	I WILL FEEL
MONDAY			
TUESDAY			
WEDNESDAY			
THURSDAY			
FRIDAY			
SATURDAY			
SUNDAY			

I feel good about myself because:

1

2

3

Have you blown up a highway with a bazooka?   ☐ YES ☐ NO

What's stressing you out right now?

What strategies do you have for shaking off the stress?

Mental Cyclists are mindful. Take Three Mental Breaths, then jot down the first 3 things you notice. These could be things you see, or hear, or smell, or feel.

1

2

3

What one change could you make to develop a more positive mindset?

You're close to your second milestone — amazing! How confident are you of success?

GOAL 1	YIKES!													YAY!
GOAL 2	YIKES!													YAY!
GOAL 3	YIKES!													YAY!

Are you winning all your willpower wars? ☐ YES ☐ NO

What is your *Yeah, But* voice telling you and how can you defeat it? _____

_____

_____

How intrinsically motivated are you to achieve your 3 goals?

GOAL 1	SHRUG													BRING IT ON!
GOAL 2	SHRUG													BRING IT ON!
GOAL 3	SHRUG													BRING IT ON!

What one change can you make to maximise your motivation? _____

_____

Mental Cyclists feel the fun. List 3 things you love about your cycling:

I LOVE _____

I LOVE _____

I LOVE _____

ABOVE ALL, BE THE HEROINE OF YOUR LIFE, NOT THE VICTIM.

NORA EPHRON, WRITER

What am I going to do this week to help me achieve my goals?

	I WILL DO	TIME	I WILL FEEL
MONDAY			
TUESDAY			
WEDNESDAY			
THURSDAY			
FRIDAY			
SATURDAY			
SUNDAY			

MILESTONE 2 | **ON THE ROAD**   DATE ....

I feel good about myself because:

1 ....

2 ....

3 ....

How committed are
you to your Mental   I'LL TRY | ┆ ┆ ┆ ┆ ┆ | ┆ ┆ ┆ ┆ ┆ | TRY STOPPING ME!
Cyclist Challenge?

Be honest about any wobbles you're having. ....

....

....

What can you do today to develop a more heroic mindset? ....

....

....

How loud is your
Cruel Critic right   SILENT | ┆ ┆ ┆ ┆ ┆ | ┆ ┆ ┆ ┆ ┆ | SCREAMING
now?

How can you squash the self-criticism? ....

....

....

Are you comparing yourself to others?   ☐ YES ☐ NO

How can you let go of this thinking? ....

....

Thinking about your Mental Cyclist Challenge, how do you feel?

- ☐ EXCITED
- ☐ STRESSED
- ☐ SCARED
- ☐ LETHARGIC
- ☐

- ☐ DETERMINED
- ☐ CALM
- ☐ SWEARY
- ☐ ENERGETIC
- ☐

- ☐ NERVOUS
- ☐ CONFIDENT
- ☐ FRUSTRATED
- ☐ UNCERTAIN
- ☐

- ☐ STRONG
- ☐ INSPIRED
- ☐ HAPPY
- ☐ WORRIED
- ☐

How is your growing self-expertise helping you hit your goals? ....

....

....

Do you want to revise any of the milestone
goals in your Route Planner?   ☐ YES ☐ NO

If so, how and why? ....

....

....

Mental Cyclists have a heroic mindset. What positive affirmations will keep you on track?

I AM ....

I CAN ....

I WILL ....

Amazing — you did it! You've reached your second milestone and you're on the home stretch now. Before you get going, take those Three Mental Breaths and notice how you feel. Give yourself a mental pat on the back. You deserve it!

To get Milestone 3 off to a flying start, make sure you are happy with your goals. If you want to make any changes, note them below so you know exactly what you've got to achieve in this final push.

GOAL 1

Why this is important

GOAL 2

Why this is important

GOAL 3

Why this is important

What am I going to do this week to help me achieve my goals?

	I WILL DO	TIME	I WILL FEEL
MONDAY			
TUESDAY			
WEDNESDAY			
THURSDAY			
FRIDAY			
SATURDAY			
SUNDAY			

How do you feel right now?

☐ EXCITED ☐ DETERMINED ☐ NERVOUS ☐ STRONG
☐ STRESSED ☐ CALM ☐ CONFIDENT ☐ SEXY
☐ SCARED ☐ POSITIVE ☐ FRUSTRATED ☐ HAPPY
☐ .... ☐ .... ☐ .... ☐ ....

Are you comparing yourself to others?   ☐ YES   ☐ NO

How can you let go of this thinking? ....

....

....

Are you winning all your willpower wars?   ☐ YES   ☐ NO

What one thing can you do to defeat your *Yeah, But* voice? ....

....

....

How extrinsically motivated are you by your 3 goals?

GOAL 1   MEH | ׀ ׀ ׀ ׀ ׀ ׀ ׀ ׀ ׀ ׀ ׀ | MASSIVELY!

GOAL 2   MEH | ׀ ׀ ׀ ׀ ׀ ׀ ׀ ׀ ׀ ׀ ׀ | MASSIVELY!

GOAL 3   MEH | ׀ ׀ ׀ ׀ ׀ ׀ ׀ ׀ ׀ ׀ ׀ | MASSIVELY!

What one change can you make to maximise your motivation? ....

....

....

Thinking about your 3 goals for this milestone, how confident are you of success?

GOAL 1   YIKES! | | | | | | | | | | | | YAY!

GOAL 2   YIKES! | | | | | | | | | | | | YAY!

GOAL 3   YIKES! | | | | | | | | | | | | YAY!

How can you adapt your goals or training to have more fun? _____

_____

Create 3 mantras using the words below, or your own. Use the I AM or YOU ARE format...

☐ STRONG   ☐ CAPABLE   ☐ FAST   ☐ LOVING IT!

☐ ENOUGH   ☐ CALM   ☐ CONFIDENT   ☐ FEARLESS

☐ A WINNER   ☐ DETERMINED   ☐ _____   ☐ _____

How will your mantras help you on your next ride? _____

_____

_____

Mental Cyclists feel the fun. List 3 things you love about your cycling:

I LOVE _____

I LOVE _____

I LOVE _____

REMEMBER WHEN YOU WERE YOUNG? YOU SHONE LIKE THE SUN.

PINK FLOYD, BAND

What am I going to do this week to help me achieve my goals?

	I WILL DO	TIME	I WILL FEEL
MONDAY			
TUESDAY			
WEDNESDAY			
THURSDAY			
FRIDAY			
SATURDAY			
SUNDAY			

I feel good about myself because:

1 ....

2 ....

3 ....

Are you aware of any true and important limiting beliefs? ☐ YES ☐ NO

How can you challenge these or work around the ones you can't change? ....

....

....

Do you perceive your milestone goals as challenges or threats?

GOAL 1 PUPPY | | | | | | | | | | | | | | | | BEAR

GOAL 2 PUPPY | | | | | | | | | | | | | | | | BEAR

GOAL 3 PUPPY | | | | | | | | | | | | | | | | BEAR

How can you move from threat to challenge? ....

....

....

How attached are you to targets? WHATEVER | | | | | | | | | | | | | | | WHATEVER IT TAKES!

How can you let go of attachment and find your flow? ....

....

....

For each goal, list one thing that could go wrong then consider how you will stay on track...

GOAL 1 IF _____

THEN _____

_____

GOAL 2 IF _____

THEN _____

_____

GOAL 3 IF _____

THEN _____

_____

What are you loving right now as you work towards your goals ? _____

_____

_____

What one change can you make to feel more fun? _____

_____

_____

Mental Cyclists have a heroic mindset. Therefore:

I AM _____

I CAN _____

I WILL _____

THE KEY TO SUCCESS IS ACTION, AND THE ESSENTIAL IN ACTION IS PERSEVERANCE.

SUN YAT–SEN, PHILOSOPHER

What am I going to do this week to help me achieve my goals?

	I WILL DO	TIME	I WILL FEEL
MONDAY			
TUESDAY			
WEDNESDAY			
THURSDAY			
FRIDAY			
SATURDAY			
SUNDAY			

DATE ....

I feel good about myself because:

1 ....

2 ....

3 ....

What's stressing you out right now? ....

....

....

What strategies do you have for shaking off the stress? ....

....

....

Mental Cyclists are mindful. Take Three Mental Breaths, then jot down the first 3 things you notice. These could be things you see, or hear, or smell, or feel.

1 ....

2 ....

3 ....

What one change could you make to develop a more positive mindset? ....

....

....

You're so close to reaching your final milestone – keep going! Thinking about what lies ahead, how do you feel?

☐ EXCITED ☐ DETERMINED ☐ NERVOUS ☐ STRONG

☐ STRESSED ☐ CALM ☐ CONFIDENT ☐ INSPIRED

☐ SCARED ☐ POSITIVE ☐ FRUSTRATED ☐ HAPPY

☐ LETHARGIC ☐ ENERGETIC ☐ WUSSY ☐ WORRIED

☐ _____ ☐ _____ ☐ _____ ☐ _____

Are you winning all your willpower wars?   ☐ YES ☐ NO

What is your *Yeah, But* voice telling you and how can you defeat it? ....

....

....

Mental Cyclists feel the fun. List 3 things you love about your cycling:

I LOVE ....

I LOVE ....

I LOVE ....

NOT TO BE IN YOUR COMFORT ZONE IS GREAT FUN.

BENEDICT CUMBERBATCH, ACTOR

What am I going to do this week to help me achieve my goals?

	I WILL DO	TIME	I WILL FEEL
MONDAY			
TUESDAY			
WEDNESDAY			
THURSDAY			
FRIDAY			
SATURDAY			
SUNDAY			

DATE ....

I feel good about myself because:

1 ....

2 ....

3 ....

Are you going to
smash your Mental   I'LL TRY | | | | | | | | | | | | | | | TRY STOPPING ME!
Cyclist Challenge?

Be honest about any wobbles you're having. ....

....

....

How loud is your
Cruel Critic right   SILENT | | | | | | | | | | | | | | | SCREAMING
now?

How can you squash the self-criticism? ....

....

....

How attached are
you to targets?   WHATEVER | | | | | | | | | | | | | | | WHATEVER IT TAKES!

How can you let go of attachment and find your flow? ....

....

....

Thinking about your Mental Cyclist Challenge, how do you feel?

☐ EXCITED ☐ DELUSIONAL ☐ NERVOUS ☐ STRONG

☐ STRESSED ☐ CALM ☐ CONFIDENT ☐ INSPIRED

☐ SCARED ☐ POSITIVE ☐ FRUSTRATED ☐ HAPPY

☐ LETHARGIC ☐ ENERGETIC ☐ UNCERTAIN ☐ WORRIED

☐ ☐ ☐ ☐

Your challenge is just around the corner. List three things that could go wrong then consider how you will stay on track...

GOAL 1 IF ....

THEN ....

....

GOAL 2 IF ....

THEN ....

....

GOAL 3 IF ....

THEN ....

....

Mental Cyclists have a heroic mindset. What positive affirmations will get your over the finish line?

I AM ....

I CAN ....

I WILL ....

Chapeau! If you've made it to this point in the book, it's likely you've completed your preparation for your Mental Cyclist Challenge. What an incredible achievement. Now get out there and smash it!

Remember to share your success to inspire others to join you on this journey — you can share your stories, tips and photos at Club TMC. Visit mentalcyclist.com to join!

Once you've completed your challenge, come back to complete this final section of the book. Enjoy taking the time to reflect on how much you've achieved as a Mental Cyclist. And remember, now you understand what you can do with the right mindset, there are no limits.

Allez!

The 3 things I'm most proud of are:

1 ....

2 ....

3 ....

What kept you motivated when things got tough? ....

....

....

Overall, how has your attitude changed since reading The Mental Cyclist? ....

....

....

....

....

....

Reflecting on your challenge, what did you love most?

I LOVED _____

I LOVED _____

I LOVED _____

3 awesome things I now know about myself as a cyclist:

1 _____

2 _____

3 _____

Got an idea for your next Mental Cyclist Challenge? Jot it down here, explaining why you're motivated to do it:

_____

_____

_____

_____

_____

_____

_____

_____

_____

_____

CHANGE YOUR MIND. CHANGE YOUR RIDE.

mentalcyclist.com

Printed in Great Britain
by Amazon

51786149R00174